Library of
Davidson College

EDUCATIONAL COMPUTER TECHNOLOGY: A MANUAL/GUIDE FOR EFFECTIVE AND EFFICIENT UTILIZATION BY SCHOOL ADMINISTRATORS

BY: BERNARD SIDMAN

PALO ALTO, CALIFORNIA
1979

PUBLISHED BY

R & E RESEARCH ASSOCIATES, INC.
936 INDUSTRIAL AVENUE
PALO ALTO, CALIFORNIA 94303

PUBLISHERS

ROBERT D. REED AND ADAM S. ETEROVICH

Library of Congress Card Catalog Number
78-68445

I.S.B.N.
0-88247-574-6

Copyright 1979
By
Bernard Sidman

TABLE OF CONTENTS

Chapter		Page
I.	BACGROUND AND RATIONALE	1
	Background of the Study	1
	Statement of the Problem	6
	Delimitations	6
	Procedures	6
II.	EFFECTIVE AND EFFICIENT UTILIZATION OF COMPUTER TECHNOLOGY BY SCHOOL ADMINISTRATORS	11
	Introduction	11
	Staff and Line Relationships -- The Computer on the Organization Chart	11
	Definition of the Concept of "System"	13
	Information Systems	15
	Educational Decision-Making	19
	Other Administrative Applications of the Computer	22
	Review of Some Existing Educational Computer Systems	25
	Summary	33
III.	DETERMINING THE FEASIBILITY OF UTILIZING COMPUTER TECHNOLOGY	40
	Introduction	40
	In-House Study or Outside Consultant	40
	Determining Data Pro-essing Needs, Goals and Objectives	42
	Organizational Analysis	45
	Feasibility Study	45
	Pros and Cons of Computerization	47
	Summary	49
IV.	PROCEDURES FOR GETTING INTO THE COMPUTER AGE	53
	Introduction	53
	Organizing the Computer Facility Team	53
	Developing the RFP	62
	Service Bureau, In-House, Time-Sharing or Consortium	63
	Evaluation and Selection of Hardware	64
	Evaluation and Selection of Software	69
	Financing: Purchase, Rental, Third Party Lease, Other	71
	Summary	75

Chapter		Page
V.	DISCUSSION AND CONCLUSIONS	79
	The Role of the Computer in Educational Administration	79
	Computer Techniques as They Relate to General Management	81
	Don't Re-Invent the Wheel	83
	Caveat Emptor	84
	BIBLIOGRAPHY	88
	APPENDICES	98
	Appendix A: Glossary of Related Terms	98
	Appendix B: EDP Chronology	118
	Appendix C: Large School System EDP Survey	128
	Appendix D: Selected Computer Companies	130
	Appendix E: Selected Magazine Listings	131
	Appendix F: Flowcharts	133
	Appendix G: Selected Educational EDP Facilities	136
	Appendix H: Request for Proposal (RFP)	137

CHAPTER 1

BACKGROUND AND RATIONALE

Background of the Study

Computer technology, unlike some other great innovations which have taken from 50 to 100 or more years to assume a meaningful role in our civilization, has in less than 30 years become an integral part of the scheme of things.[1] Moreover, unlike most other great inventions which usually are a boon to a select industry or group of industries, computer technology has established itself as being almost indispensable in most human activities.[2] This being the case, it seems rather odd that the level of utilization of this technology by school administrators has, for the most part, been rather minimal. It would appear that this low level of utilization is due, to a great extent, to the fact that too few educators understand computer technology. Goodlad et al. pointed out that "many educational practitioners do not relish the prospect of automation" and that "there is also a serious lack of knowledge on the part of educators about the power and potential of computer systems for improving educational programs."[3] Educators have demonstrated time and again a proclivity not to be the first to try any new technology until its feasibility is demonstrated by someone else. Since both the feasibility and the applicability of the use of computers has been demonstrated by some forward thinking school administrators, the lack of knowledge and action on the part of the majority of school administrators is inexcusable.

Educational administrators should realize that they can use the computer not only as a tool but also as a force for change.[4] Actually, "the uses of the computer and EDP in the administration of public education are limited only by the imagination of professional administrators."[5] Even the simplest of applications of computer technology (e.g., student attendance, student class scheduling, student grade reporting, payroll, accounting, budgeting, personnel inventory, facilities inventory and transportation) will allow for a more efficient and effective utilization of both personnel and facilities. All of these applications require a rather low level of effort to become fully operational. Though these applications seem to utilize the computer only as a tool, with a little work they can also be used to experiment with varying patterns of staffing, student scheduling patterns and projecting possible future needs thus utilizing the computer to supply information vital to decision-making relative to potential changes in the educational system.

The administrator should be aware that the computer is completely neutral throughout this entire process. The computer does, basically, only what it is told (programmed) to do; the administrator not the computer makes decisions.[6] Hansen expressed the same thought by stating, "one of the purposes for installation of a computer is to furnish management with pertinent data to make better decisions."[7] Tondow addressing this point in an even firmer manner said, "the capability of an institution to individualize, to offer accurate and relevant information, to have flexibility of organization and to have a posture toward change all requires, and is dependent upon, its computer capabilities."[8]

The computer is a device which, if properly utilized, not only affects the administrative processes relative to the better performance of house keeping functions and the routine information gathering tasks but the machine also provides the administrator with time and information thus allowing him to become a more competent and effective educational leader.[9] In spite of all the evidence attesting to the above,[10] the world of education (in general) has not achieved notable success with computer technology *per se*. It would seem that the fault lies in the failure on the part of administrators to place change and innovation at the heart of operating procedures.[11] This is not to suggest that educators immediately jump upon each and every new bandwagon which appears, but rather that innovation and change should not be avoided simply because of an innate fear of the hitherto unknown.

It is an unamusing paradox that exists since administration in an educational setting is a process of managing and conducting a program of activities that facilitates the teaching and learning process and yet it refuses to employ all information sources that could enhance this process.[12] This reluctance by school administrators can be blamed partially upon the computer companies who, upon realizing the potential market which the school systems represented, flooded the public schools with detailed technical data such as: It has a core storage capacity of either 4K, 8K, 16K, 32K, etc., in terms of 16-bit words each of which is equivalent to two 8-bit bytes. Obviously then the indicated K of core is actually twice as much compared to some other company that only uses an 8-bit word. Moreover, since the CPU has a core-storage cycle time of 2.2 microseconds and a single platter two surface randomly accessible disk with 512K words of additional storage, it must be quite clear to you, Mr. Administrator, that our equipment is precisely what you need. This type of information only served to boggle the mind with irrelevant and unnecessary information.

There is no need for the educator to comprehend the inner workings of a computer, but what he must have is an understanding of what this machine, in conjunction with other electronic devices, can and cannot do.[13] The lack of flow of meaningful information, of which the above is but one example, is interesting in that it points out the need for some sort of mechanism that will place meaningful data in the hands of administrators to allow them to make reasonable decisions relative to their potential utilization of computer technology. It is also interesting from the point of view that the lack of flow of total information that also exists within the educator's own school system is precisely one of the problems that computer technology will help to eliminate.

An educational computer system is designed specifically to help the user in securing the exact information he seeks and also in analyzing, annotating and predicting possible alternative roads to his goals.[14] This potential is presently available at a time when there is, according to Castetter, "hardly an administrator who will admit that he can secure, at any time and in proper form, the essential information he needs for the conduct of his work."[15] This situation need not exist. The fact that it does exist offers further evidence of the lack of familiarity that educational administrators have with computer technology as it relates to effective and efficient school administration.

Educational computer technology is certainly not the panacea for all of the administrators' problems. But it can provide the school system with the specific and general information needed to deal with both internal and external problems.[16] Unfortunately, even those school systems that utilize computer technology often do so in a most rudimentary manner.

Gott has found that "only a small minority of educational institutions succeed in getting the benefit they expect to gain from a computer installation at the price they expect to pay, much less reach their EDP goals on schedule."[17] Some of the reasons for this expensive tragedy are: improper placement of the computer manager on the organizational chart; lack of understanding of information systems and their relationship to educational decision-making; purchase of inappropriate hardware and/or software; improper assessment of the feasibility of utilizing computer technology at this point in time; and numerous others. All of these factors need to be examined to learn how to cope with them in the hope of removing them from the list of potential roadblocks to the successful utilization of educational computer technology. They should be dealt with in simple language using fully explained computer jargon only when it seems relevant to do so.

To further assist the administrator to properly utilize computer technology, there is also a need to review certain common elements that are nearly always present in those school systems which have had a successful computer effort e.g., identification of key service objectives, identification of potential applications, preparation of long range application plans, analysis of alternative applications for trade-offs, preparation of comprehensive implementation plans, regular monitoring by top management of progress and performance, conducting of a formal evaluation of the computer services effort and continuous inservice training programs.[18] All of this information has as yet to be compiled, written in layman's terminology and presented in a single work to assist the administrator.

There is a growing demand by state legislatures and by school boards for school corporations to implement systems of accountability and management by objectives. The state of Indiana, for example, has mandated that the school corporations shall implement PPBS (Planning Programming Budgeting System) by September, 1976. It will become obvious, if it already hasn't, that a school corporation without the advantage of having access to a computer system will either find it impossible to comply with this law or will do so at a tremendous expense of both manpower and money. Another interesting side of this situation will be the manner in which those educational administrators with their own computer systems actually carry out this implementation. Will they follow all the state's suggestions on how to get into PPBS and then plug the system into their computers as one more program? Or will the administrators' PPB system be properly merged into their total computerized management information system -- if one exists? It is likely that for most school corporations that a computerized management system of any form is neither in existence nor are its structure or potential understood by the administrators. We would be hard pressed to find many school corporations using computer technology to simulate new spending or financing plans, new forms of organization or in any other new and imaginative method of educational simulation to assist in the decision-making process.[19] This is in no way to be construed as a measure of the competence of the school administrator but rather as an indication of the "growing need for a literature of experience providing blow-by-blow accounts of how forward looking states and school districts have resolved these difficulties . . . and other problems in setting up automated school information processing systems."[20] For some strange reason there seems to be a lack of communications amongst educators relative to their success or failure, and the reasons thereof, in utilizing computer technology. It may very well be that there is "no right way" to develop the efficient and effective utilization of computer technology in an education institution,[21] but a knowledge of how it has been done in other places and of the similarities that may or may not exist in staff, facilities, funds and the types of equipment available will certainly give the administrator a meaningful data base from which to select the best path to follow. The point being that if the administrator is a competent educator who has expertise in his profession, then he can acquire the necessary technical skills to properly utilize computer technology. What is needed, according to Hansen, is not more sophisticated electronic equipment but rather a "requirement for training professional and support personnel within the educational institutions to use even our existing computer technology."[22]

The plea for educational administrators to obtain a level of competence or familiarity with computer technology is not new. A 1967 report from the American Association of School Administrators (AASA) contained the following:

The AASA Committee on Electronic Data Processing states unequivocally that one of the important professional talents for an administrator today is proficiency in the use and direction of electronic data processing, software and hardware.

The creative adaptation of electronic data processing to school administration is long overdue. The superintendent who continues to ignore the computer does so at his own peril.[23]

It is strongly urged by the AASA Committee on Electronic Data Processing that all institutions of higher learning presently preparing school administrators develop adequately staffed programs and obtain access to computer hardware necessary for creating high skill levels among future and present school administrators in the comprehension and use of computer systems.

It would be highly desirable to have all present administrative practitioners gain a working understanding of EDP in as short a time as possible.[24]

Gott and Gengwish four years later took the same position when they stated that "for the public schools superintendent to operate his district effectively and efficiently in the seventies, he needs certain basic knowledge of computers -- the hardware and the software."[25] Gott and Gengwish elaborated further that:

Armed with an understanding of the major operational concepts and the more significant mechanical and operational characteristics of computer systems, the superintendent will be in a position to evaluate proposals for computer installations and to ask appropriate questions concerning the capabilities and limitations of various computer "packages." For detailed and specific information, the superintendent may rely on his data processing systems staff, representatives of computer manufacturers, and various trade and technical publications. The important concern is that the superintendent is able to ask intelligent questions -- and that can come only after he has gained a general knowledge of computer systems and of the relationship between hardware, software and cost.[26]

An even stronger position was taken three years later in 1974, when Alan B. Ellis began his book The Use and Misuse of Computers in Education on the premise that since "educators are unclear and confused about what computers are, hence frequently misuse them."

These last few comments along with the preceding information about the present state of the utilization of computer technology in educational administration, presents a rather definitive case for educators with computer skills to communicate (in layman's language) with their peers in an attempt to enable more educational administrators to obtain some familiarity with computer technology -- software and hardware -- as it relates to effective and efficient school administration.

Statement of the Problem

The purpose of this study was to develop a body of information to enable educational administrators to obtain familiarity with computer technology as it relates to effective and efficient school administration. This was accomplished by a critical analysis of meaningful experiences, alternatives and/or solutions to the following questions:

1. What is effective and efficient utilization of computer technology by school administrators?

2. When is a school system ready for computer technology?

3. What are the procedures for incorporating computer technology?

Delimitations

There is a plethora of literature on computer technology that is presently available. In order to present the broadest range of possible alternatives and/or solutions to the problem being studied, titles were selected on the basis of their potential relevance to this study from fields other than education as well as from the field of education.

Within the field of education, a major portion of the writing has been done about the use of the computer as an instructional tool. This is an area which presents many facets such as computer-assisted instruction (CAI), computer managed instruction (CMI), computer based education (CBE) and computer assisted test construction (CATC) any of which is worthy of an entire study. However, the present study will deal only with applications of the computer as an administrative tool and its applicability in areas such as pupil services, personnel services, finances, facilities, planning-control-evaluation, research, program evaluation and review technique (PERT), planning-programming-budgeting system (PPBS), simulation, linear programming and management information systems.

Procedures

The procedures used to obtain the information contained

in this study included: a literature research, correspondence and data collection (relative to hardware configurations and software available for educational management systems) from different computer companies (see Appendix D) and visitations to ongoing educational EDP facilities. (See Appendix G)

The literature relative to this study was identified in: an extensive bibliography compiled by the Massachusetts Educational Data Processing Association, an ERIC computer search, and from readings in various technical and trade journals. Data were also requested from computer companies which were listed in the computer systems section of the Computerworld Stock Trading Summary, (Computerworld the Newsweekly for the Computer Community, Newton, Massachusetts, August 21, 1974, p. 55). The educational EDP facilities visited included equipment from the following companies: Digital Equipment Corporation (DEC), International Business Machines (IBM), Honeywell and National Cash Register (NCR).

Each of these sources was investigated to obtain information on: (1) the various aspects of what constitutes the effective and efficient utilization of computer technology - this was discerned by a critical analysis of the concepts of system and information systems along with the process of educational decision-making and various other educational administrative applications of computer technology, (2) the methods and techniques involved in performing a feasibility study to determine the pros and cons of computerization and the feasibility of utilizing computer technology and (3) various approaches to computerization such as service bureaus, consortiums, time-sharing or in-house systems and the process of obtaining information about and evaluating a potential in-house system.

The topics mentioned above are the focal points for this study. The remainder of this thesis is structured to deal with the information and data related to those specific points. Chapter II discusses (1) the concepts of system and information systems as they relate to educational decision-making, (2) presents an overview of existing system technology and potential administrative applications of the computer, (3) reviews some existing on-going educational computer systems, (4) analyses staff and line relationships to determine where the computer belongs on the organization chart and (5) by analysis of the present state of computer technology and the existing utilization of computers in educational administration, determines how school administrators can utilize computer technology as an effective and efficient administrative tool. Chapter III discusses the rationale and techniques necessary to study an educational system to determine the feasibility of utilizing computer technology by either conducting an in-house study or by hiring an outside consultant to: (1) determine the organization's needs, goals and objectives, (2) analyze the existing organization to determine a structure that will allow for the implementation of an effective and efficient management system and (3) present both the pros and cons of trying to utilize computer technology as an administrative tool. Chapter IV discusses some of the procedures for evaluating the various methods of employing computer technology such as: (1) developing the Request for Proposal (RFP) to insure receipt of meaningful bids, (2) determining the best means of acquiring computer technology -- service bureau, consortium, time-sharing or having an in-house system, (3) evaluation and selection of both hardware and software if an in-house computer system is desired and (4) various methods of financing a computer system -- straight purchase, rental or third party lease. Chapter V presents a summary and recapitulation of the role of the computer in educational administration along with a warning relative to some of the dangers and pitfalls that other educators have encountered in their efforts to utilize computer technology.

FOOTNOTES -- CHAPTER I

[1] Burck, Gilbert, and the editors of Fortune, *The Computer Age*, p. 6.

[2] *Ibid.*, p. 7.

[3] Goodland, J. I., et al., *Computers and Information Systems in Education*, pp. 28-29.

[4] Wilson, M. J., *Cybernetics and Education: A Colloquium*, p. ix.

[5] *EDP and the School Administrator*, American Association of School Administrators, 1967, p. viii.

[6] Floyd, J. D., *The Computer: An Administrative Dilemma*, pp. 10-11.

[7] Hansen, Burdette, "The Computer and Management Information in Education Related Organizations," *Educational Technology*, p. 15.

[8] Louchary, J. W., and Tondow, Mrray, editors, *Educational Information System Requirements: The Next Two Decades*, p. 11.

[9] *Ibid.*, pp. 80, 84.

[10] Chapter II will document much of this evidence.

[11] Cumming, W. K., "Educational Administration for Systems Technology and Innovations," *AEDS Journal*, June, 1972, p. 112.

[12] Floyd, *op. cit.*, p. 1.

[13] Goodland, *op. cit.*, p. 93.

[14] Cumming, *op. cit.*, p. 114.

[15] Castetter, W. B., *The Personnel Function in Educational Administration*, p. 78.

[16] Handy, H. W., et al., *The Computer in Education*, p. 6.

[17] Gott, John, and Gengwish, Nick, "What the Public Schools Superintendent Needs to Know About Computer Hardware and Sofeware," *AEDS Monitor*, October, 1971, p. 8.

[18] *Ibid.*, p. 8.

[19] Smith, R. C., *The AEDS Large School System Survey. Report of Findings*, p. 3.

[20] Goodland, *op. cit.*, p. 103.

[21] Tondow, Murray, "Computers in the Schools: Palo Alto," *Datamation*, June, 1968, p. 62.

[22] Hansen, D. N., *The Role of Computers in Education During the 70's*, p. 1.

[23] *EDP and the School Administrator*, op. cit., p. x.

[24] *Ibid.*, pp. 40-41.

[25] Gott and Gengwish, op. cit., p. 8.

[26] *Ibid.*, p. 9.

CHAPTER 2

EFFECTIVE AND EFFICIENT UTILIZATION OF COMPUTER
TECHNOLOGY BY SCHOOL ADMINISTRATORS

Introduction

The effective and efficient utilization of any tool or technique is usually a function of the user's familiarity with its operational capabilities and characteristics. This familiarity could be developed over a period of time using a method of trial and error. However, it is most inefficient and uneconomical for similar groups (educational administrators) using similar tools (computer technology) to use a method of trial and error to eventually develop quite similar procedures. The lack of widespread demonstration and dissemination of results achieved by successful educational data processing installations is probably one of the most important reasons for the slow diffusion of computer technology applications into education.[1] This lack of communication is most unfortunate especially in light of Robin C. Smith's large school system survey which found that ". . . there is sufficient common-ground among school districts to allow the transfer and enhancement of application software."[2] Another reason for inefficient utilization of computer technology in educational administration is that ". . . to a great extent, operational school personnel do not know what computers and data processing systems can do for them in helping to solve their problems."[3]

It seems essential that school administrators be aware of the successes that some of their peers are having in utilizing computer technology as an administrative tool. The potential for transferring these successes to ones' own school corporation, however, requires at least a minimal level of understanding of the concepts of "system" and "information systems" and the relative position of a computer department within the organizational structure. This information, combined with an awareness of the many applications of computer technology being employed by existing educational computer centers, will enable the educational administrator to pursue a more logical course of action as he attempts to implement and utilize a computer system in his corporation.

Staff and Line Relationships -- The Computer on the Organization Chart

Some of the reasons for the success or lack of success achieved by administrators trying to use computer technology can be found in the position of the computer center on the organization chart. Placing a computer facility in a position where its products are influenced or controlled by a specific application area, e.g., finance, student personnel, facilities, etc..., invariably tends to make it a slave to that function.[4] The AASA Committee on Electronic Data Processing (EDP) recognized this danger in 1967 when they reported that ". . . EDP should be planned and coordinated to satisfy a unified pattern of information needs of the school district rather than to fit a specific application in only some segment of the total educational operation."[5] The report went on to say that ". . . to confine the computer to such pedestrian uses, that is, to clerical, routine, or logistical purposes, would be to limit attainment of its full potential."[6]

Unfortunately, there have been too many instances where the computer has been utilized (or rather deutilized) in such a restricted manner. Robin C. Smith in his large school survey of 61 districts of 40,000 or more pupils each, found that emphasis is placed primarily on the "bread and butter" applications in the financial and personnel areas e.g., general expenditure accounting, accounts receivable, payroll, budget development and employee data base.[7] The main reason for this narrow use of the potential of the computer is that all too often, at least initially, the computer center is placed on the organization chart so that its director reports to the administrator in charge of business and/or finance. It is just such an improper organizational structure that prompted the AASA committee to recommend in 1967 "that the management, control, and evaluation of EDP be delegated to an administrative position qualified to serve the EDP needs of the school district as a whole."[8] It is also essential that "the director of such a system should be responsible directly to a top administrator."[9] Handy et al., were even more explicit as to the structure of the organization chart when they indicated that the head of the computer center should have cabinet status and that he should report directly to the superintendent of schools.[10]

It should be quite clear by this time that the position of the computer on the organization chart plays an important part in determining whether or not the system will be utilized in an effective and efficient manner. There seems to be no question that there should be a qualified individual responsible for the activities of the computer center and that he should be placed within the organization so that he reports directly to the superintendent of schools. Bruce Alcorn, in his article "The Concept of Total Systems in Education," summed up the importance of the position of the computer center on the organizational chart when he wrote that

> Placing the top administrator of the information system next to the top executive of the educational institution is extremely important . . . this also places the burden of serving all segments equally, and in an integrated manner, where it belongs.[11]

Definition of the Concept of "System"

Unlike the technological innovations that they could represent, the terms system and systems analysis have become quite an accepted part of the administrator's vocabulary. Oettinger noted that "to some extent, speaking of systems is little more than appealing to a fashionable metaphor for the sake of snowing someone."[12] The use of fashionable jargon without really understanding what it means is by no means limited to educational administrators.

There are many phrases which contain the word system(s). However, an understanding of the word system and of the phrase systems analysis (also called systems approach) would allow one to decipher, or at least have a general idea, of the meanings of the myriad of other expressions/titles which contain the word system(s). There are many ways of explaining any concept and of interpreting the explanation once it is given. The following material is being presented in the hope that it will contain at least one explanation each for "system" and "systems analysis" to enable the reader to feel comfortable with his understanding of these terms.

Systems

An assemblage of objects united by some form of regular interaction or interdependence; an organic or organized whole.[13]

A regularly interacting or interdependent group of items forming a unified whole.[14]

An assembly of components united by some form of regulated interaction to form an organized whole.[15]

An assembly of procedures, processes, methods, routines, or techniques united by some form of regulated interaction to form an organized whole.[16]

By system we mean a set of interrelated factors that are used together to produce an outfit . . . in all of these systems there are various ways of combining the elements or inputs in order to produce outputs.[17]

A system is an orderly combination of interrelated and interacting parts which constitute a rational whole and which create a functional and organizational Gestalt through the purpose and collective effort of the separate parts working independently and in interaction to achieve previously specified performance objectives.[18]

> . . . the concept of system -- a set of interacting units with spatial as well as temporal boundaries.[19]

> . . . a collection of interdependent parts belonging to a hierarchy in which a system may have subsystems of its own while acting as a mere part of a suprasystem.[20]

A careful reading of the above definitions clearly illustrates how a simple term such as system can spawn an entirely new vocabulary e.g., input, output, subsystem, suprasystem, etc. Moreover, as the literature relating to a particular concept grows and becomes more widely disseminated, the potential for application of the original concept grows as well as the concept itself. An example of this is Pilecki's contention that any given school, or school district, is actually a system because: (1) it has incoming energies (inputs), (2) is organized into a structure of processes and controls (functioning subsystems), (3) yields energies to the larger, or, suprasystem (outputs), (4) it is bounded spatially by other institutions which are non-schools and (5) it is encased in the limitations of time.[21] The true value of being able to identify something as a system lies in the hope that as such it will be responsive to the new concepts of technology and management that have been developed relative to systems per se.

Systems Analysis/Approach

> Systems analysis, in the simplest terms is a method of analyzing by list the desired objectives and available resources, then determining the alternative methods of using these resources to gain the objectives. The systems approach also involves looking at a problem as a whole and dealing with the interplay between parts of the problem as well as with the parts themselves. Rand thinkers call this approach "applied common sense" but sometimes it leads to a basic instructing of key problems.[22]

> The examination of an activity, procedure, method, technique, or a business to determine what must be accomplished and how the necessary operations may best be accomplished.[23]

With Sippl's definition of systems analysis in mind, it should seem obvious to any competent school administrator that the Rand Corporation's comment that the systems approach technique is nothing more than "applied common sense" is certainly apropos. However, a common sense approach to a problem will usually provide desirable results only if one also has a thorough understanding of the components which make up the problem. Also, familiarity with the available related technology and tools which might be utilized will allow for a more judicial use of one's common sense in a problem solving situation.

According to Oettinger there are at least three conditions which must be satisfied to meaningfully employ the systems approach:

1. The system being studied must be independent enough of the systems which combine with it to form a suprasystem (simply a larger system containing all other systems being examined) for interactions among these systems to be either satisfactorily accounted for or else ignored without dire consequences.

2. The system being studied must be one for which well-developed and proved research and design tools exist.

3. When designing a system, one must know explicitly what it is for.[24]

Silvern defined the systems approach as a process consisting of four major parts: analysis, synthesis, modeling and simulation. According to him:

> . . . analysis is performed on existing information to identify the problem, identify existing elements and identify the interrelationships; __synthesis__ is performed to combine unrelated elements and relationships into a new whole which is initially information; __models__ are constructed which can predict effectiveness before actual implementation of the system; __simulation__ is performed which reveals alternative solutions.[25]

The use of the systems approach, as described above, implies that: a study of the objectives of the organization will be done; a study of the available related technology and tools will be done and a determination will be made of the detail and organization of information for prudent decision making. The underlying implication is that at its best, the systems approach will solve problems far more satisfactorily than naked intuition/common sense.[26]

Information Systems

There are many ways of describing "information systems." However, it seems that a working knowledge of what an information system is can be obtained quickly by (1) simple definitions and (2) presenting both its major objectives and its component parts.

In its most basic form, an information system is nothing more than a planned method of collecting meaningful data and then converting it to summaries[27] and other reports that serve some vital purpose in the organization's program. These systems can be powered by hand (manual systems) or by machine (automated systems).[28] The information systems used for administrative purposes are commonly referred to as either a management information system (MIS), a total management information system (TMIS) or a total information system (TIS). A TIS is also referred to as an integrated system.

Van Dusseldorp defines an MIS as "an organized method of providing management with information needed for decisions, when it is needed and in a form which aids understanding and stimulates action."[29] Notice that there is no mention of computers in this definition. Gothe, however, defines an MIS as "a set of computerized processes that provides, in a timely manner, the information necessary to support decision making."[30] Though Gothe uses the term "computerized" in his definition and Van Dusseldorp does not, their definitions are still basically the same.

The major objectives of an MIS are summarized rather succinctly by both Bumsted and Foley. To provide an opportunity for comparison both men's models are presented. Bumsted summarizes the major objectives as:

1. Provide data to assure adequate managerial direction and control of all aspects of the educational system.

2. Provide evaluative assistance in the analysis of educational programs and concepts as well as of program implementation.

3. Be responsive to, and facilitate revisions brought about by improvements, requirement changes and technological advances.

4. Afford an ongoing evaluation of the MIS itself.

5. Provide a medium for the dissemination of information and interdepartmental communication.[31]

While Foley summarized them as:

1. To provide data related to system operation for administration direction and control of change.

2. To provide for the collection, organization and storage of data relative to programs and goals of the system.

3. To provide for the analysis and evaluative procedures and techniques for program implementation, operation and termination.

4. To provide a response capability for the facilitation of change and revision of programs and procedures.

5. To provide for an ongoing evaluation of the MIS system.

6. To provide for the communication of information within and without the system.[32]

The component parts of an MIS represent the reservoirs of information that the system acts upon in fulfilling its major objectives. For an educational management information system the basic component parts, commonly referred to as the "data base", would include files (lists of information) on at least each of the following (all of which will be dealt with in greater detail in succeeding sections): (1) finance -- all cost elements relative to the educational program, (2) staff -- includes demographic characteristics, training and experience, ratings and effectiveness measures and salary, (3) facility -- includes site characteristics, the buildings (construction, age and condition), the educational and non-educational space, the equipment specifications and program materials, (4) pupil -- includes demographic characteristics, measures of intelligence and achievement, all school records, (5) community and (6) transportation.[33] Ideally, comprehensive catalogs in each of these areas would be available for use in the development and implementation of an operational educational MIS.[34]

At this point, it should be obvious that the creation and, hopefully, the utilization of the above educational data base is an ideal application for the computer with its ability to store and retrieve data. However, the most effective and efficient utilization of the computer in this system is accomplished by building ties or links between the component parts to make them dynamic rather than static files. In this way, a data base will allow for the representation of the interrelatedness of events in the system.[35] For an MIS to be totally integrated i.e., become a total information system (TIS), all of the procedural and informational segments would be organized either as one common data bank or as a series of data banks that are readily cross-referenceable. For example, assume that there is a segment that contains the transportation file and that there is another segment that contains the pupil attendance file. An addition or deletion of a pupil to the attendance file may have an affect upon the transportation file. If so, then under a TIS, a change in the attendance file would automatically trigger an update (the appropriate change) to the transportation file (along with whatever other files that might be affected).

The development of an information system should always be done with a view toward its ultimate operational principles. The State Department of Education for South Carolina summarized these principles as:

1. <u>Master File Storage and Maintenance</u>: Storage of

master files of information are maintained as near the source as practical, and where they are most useful, as a part of the day-to-day operations, and where updating is a result of performing these operations.[36]

2. <u>Procedures for Data Transmission</u>: The system must provide for the transmission of data to those who need the information in carrying out education related responsibilities.

3. <u>Diminishing Detail</u>: With movement upward through administrative levels, less detailed information is required -- the school district requires a smaller number of detailed items of information than does the school; the State education agency requires a smaller number than the school district; etc.

4. <u>Economy of Data Collection</u>: The system must yield a maximum of unduplicated information in each contact with a data source.

5. <u>Compatibility</u>: Items of data in an educational information system must be compatible to facilitate comparisons. This is accomplished by uniformity of terminology, definitions, concepts and procedures.

6. <u>Data Item Selection</u>: An item to be included in an educational information system must meet one or more of the following criteria.

   a. Provide a basis for decision-making related to the management and direction of the education enterprise.

   b. Assist in the performance of regulatory, legislative and congressional functions.

   c. Aid in the evaluation of the effectiveness of educational programs.

   d. Be useful in the teaching -- learning process.

   e. Help inform the public about education.

7. <u>Commitment</u>: Development and maintenance of an educational information system is dependent upon a commitment at top administrative levels to the optimum use of machines and human effort.

8. <u>Confidentiality</u>: The privacy and rights of individuals, i.e., pupils, staff, school board mem-

bers, etc., must be protected.[37]

Whether the information system is an MIS or a TIS, it is bound to be limited by the objectives of the organization and the resources allocated for the system. Therefore, commitment to a systems approach (hopefully TIS) and the effective utilization of computers in an educational organization demand that the superintendent recognize, in the beginning, that the administrative structure and organizational policies, to which information system personnel relate, must be such as to make possible the orderly development, maintenance and control of procedures to promote the free flow of information throughout the organization: horizontally across conventional administrative lines, and vertically between the highest and lowest level of users, whether administrators, researchers, teachers or students.[38] The vertical and horizontal integration through the TIS will eliminate organizational isolation and allow for closer interaction of all the component parts. Hopefully, if properly structured, an educational information system will meet its ultimate objective of providing meaningful data required for prudent decisions when and where needed and within the shortest possible time.

Educational Decision-Making

At the outset it should be emphatically noted that it is the educational administrator and not the computerized MIS that ultimately makes management decisions. The key-word in the phrase "management information system", as it relates to decision-making, is "information". As we have already seen, one of the main objectives of an MIS is to provide information that is needed to stimulate prudent decision-making, not information just for the sake of information i.e., meaningless reams of computer printouts.[39]

Some of the more obvious problems that educational administrators face in their decision-making process are: (1) inaccessible relevant information, (2) an excess of irrelevant information, (3) insufficient funds to obtain the needed information, (4) not knowing whether or not the information required is available and (5) not being able to get the necessary information in a desired or understandable format.[40] Using the TIS concept, school administrators can eliminate many information problems (the above included), increase the quality of their decisions, more effectively evaluate problems and become more accountable for resources and accomplishments.[41] However, even with an integrated management information system, the educational administrator cannot always function effectively within the continual-change environment of public school education as created by the demands of a knowledge-based society. But there are certain techniques that, if put to use via the computerized TIS, would provide a greater range of alternatives and thus promote greater efficiency in educational management.[42] These techniques are commonly referred to as decision-science techniques. Five such techniques are: PERT (program evaluation and review technique),

PPBS (planning, programming, budgeting system), simulation, linear programming (LP) and projection techniques. The following brief definitions and/or examples are presented simply to create an awareness of the application of decision-science techniques to educational decision-making.[43]

PERT

PERT has wide application in the scheduling and sequencing of events that are associated with any complex projects such as constructing a school facility, developing a new curriculum, developing a manual of school policies, etc. This technique can often help in realizing a savings in both the time and cost required to complete a given project.

PPBS

PPBS is more than a budgeting/accounting system. It is actually a system of management by objectives (MBO) under which the various functions of an organization are broken down into their component parts and then assessed to determine what service it should provide. As much as possible, the amounts of service should be measurable both by contribution to the overall objective of the function and also by their cost to the overall organization. Incorporating a PPBS approach into their computerized total information system (TIS), a school corporation could easily determine (1) whether or not the specific objectives of a particular curricular program had been met and (2) the various costs (as well as the total cost) e.g., salaries, fringe benefits, facilities, materials, equipment, etc., associated with a particular program.

Simulation

The *Computer Dictionary and Handbook* defines simulation as, "The experimental technique of an operating system by means of mathematical or physical models that operate on real world or specifically devised problems in a time -- sequential method similar to the system itself." A somewhat simpler definition is that of Mize and Cox:

> We shall use simulation to mean the process of conducting experiments on a model of a system in lieu of either (1) direct experimentation with the system itself, or (2) direct analytical solution of some problem associated with the system. A system is a set of objects united by some form of interaction or interdependence. A model is a representation of the real system. An experiment is the process of observing the performance of the system or its model under a certain set of conditions.[44]

The main purpose of this technique is to allow the decision-maker to play the "what if" game i.e., what would happen if certain factors relative to the system are changed? A very simple example would be trying to arrive at an acceptable student-teacher ratio by (1) estimating next year's enrollment, (2) given the budget situation, estimate the number of teachers you will be able to have on the staff and (3) then actually figure out the student-teacher ratio. Even in this simple case, the factors of (1) student enrollment, (2) number of teachers (3) salary of teachers and (4) total budget could be manipulated separately or in combinations to arrive at various student-teacher ratios. If one had a preconceived idea of an acceptable student-teacher ratio, the factors (1), (2), (3) and (4) could be mathematically manipulated by a computer simulation to arrive at many alternative patterns all of which would yield the desired student-teacher ratio.

Linear Programming

According to Mathews, "applications of linear programming in educational decision-making are found primarily in educational finance, personnel compensation, and evaluation of instructional programs."[45] Other phases of educational administration and management that are suited to the use of linear programming include determining minimum foundation support from the state, developing salary schedules, curriculum construction and revision, schedule-making, cafeteria menu planning, developing school bus routes, establishing school attendance zones and forecasting school construction needs.[46]

Projection Techniques

Many of the things done via linear programming, especially those that involve forecasting, can be done by statistical projection techniques that do not depend upon linear programming. Perhaps a few of the most obvious examples are student enrollment, facility utilization/needs and future staffing requirements.

As stated earlier, these decision-science techniques were presented simply to create an awareness of some effective and efficient ways of utilizing a computerized educational total management information system. Incorporating some of these techniques into a well designed educational administrative computer system along with good systems management, sophisticated use of its outputs and practical/effective methods of collection and dissemination of information will help eliminate what Bumsted refers to as the schools "exponential spiral into administrative and educational confusion."[47]

Other Administrative Applications of the Computer

A myriad of administrative computer applications have been, and are constantly being developed both by school systems all over the country and by private enterprises. The list that follows represents a sample of some of the computer applications presently being used by educational administrators.[48]

A. <u>Pupil Applications</u>

1. Pupil Data Base
   a. Demographic data

2. Attendance Reporting
   a. Daily absence lists
   b. Attendance reports with appropriate statistics i.e., daily, weekly, monthly, . . ., quarterly, . . ., yearly
   c. State attendance register with appropriate demographic data and statistics
   d. Attendance/absence pattern analysis
   e. Record of new pupils
   f. Record of dropouts
   g. School building/district membership summaries by age, grade, etc.
   h. School system census
   i. Gummed labels for permanent record cards

3. Grade Reporting
   a. Report cards with present and cumulative attendance
   b. Warning notices
   c. Failure list
   d. Honor roll list
   e. Grade distribution and frequency for class, individual teachers and individual departments
   f. Current and cumulative credits
   g. Rank in class
   h. Quality point average
   i. Transcripts
   j. Gummed labels for permanent record cards

4. Course Scheduling
   a. Flexible and comprehensive scheduling options to meet the needs of the individual school
   b. Some reports generated upon successful completion of scheduling process

      i. Individual student schedules
      ii. Class rosters
      iii. Homeroom rosters
      iv. Study hall rosters
      v. Teacher utilization
      vi. Room utilization

        vii. Period utilization
        viii. Course master list and tally
        ix. Gummed labels for permanent record cards

5. Miscellaneous
   a. Test scoring (teacher made and standardized) and analysis
   b. Pupil registration
   c. Pupil census
   d. Enrollment forecasting
   e. Health and immunization records
   f. Guidance and counseling records
   g. Locker assignments
   h. Bus tickets
   i. Co-curricular activities
   j. Work experience

B. <u>Financial Applications</u>

1. Personnel Accounting
   a. Annual budgeted salary
   b. Payroll register
   c. Check printing
   d. Year-to-date register
   e. Local, state and federal reports
      i. Social security, W-2 forms, unemployment benefits, etc.
   f. Teacher annuities
   g. Personnel reports
   h. Weekly time sheets
   i. Labor distribution reports

2. Encumbrance Accounting
   a. Vendor master list
   b. Budget transaction report
   c. Cash listing
   d. Purchase order transaction listing
   e. Detailed budget report
   f. Cash statement
   g. Invoice listing
   h. Bill list
   i. Check register
   j. Check/warrant printing
   k. Open vendor listing
   l. Vendor master file maintenance report

3. Accounts Receivable

4. Job Cost Accounting

5. School Lunch Income and Expenditure Accounting

6. General Budget Preparation/Accounting

C. <u>Personnel Applications</u>

    1. Employee Data Base
       a. Demographic data

    2. Position Control

    3. Recruitment and Hiring

    4. Certification

    5. Inservice Training

    6. Employee Retirement

    7. Substitute Teachers

    8. Salary Information

    9. Employment record
       a. Absenteeism, leaves-of-absence, sabbaticals, etc.

    10. Evaluations

D. <u>Instructional/Non-Instructional Material Applications</u>

    1. Instructional Materials Inventory

    2. Instructional Materials Booking and Scheduling

    3. Library and Textbook Ordering

    4. Warehouse Inventory and Requisitioning

    5. Purchasing

    6. Instructional Materials Catalogues

    7. School Lunch Planning, Ordering and Inventory

E. <u>Facilities and Equipment Applications</u>

    1. Facilities Inventory

    2. Facilities Construction Project Control

    3. Work Order Request Scheduling

    4. Bus Scheduling and Routing

    5. Equipment Inventory

    6. Preventive Maintenance Schedule

            7. Facilities Utilization and Evaluation

            8. Equipment Utilization and Evaluation

            9. Future Facilities Planning

    F. Community Characteristics

        1. Identification Data
            a. Grid, political, geographic, postal, administrative, zoning, sheets, etc.

        2. Facilities and Services
            a. Recreational, cultural, law enforcement, fire protection, health/welfare facilities, transportation

        3. Socioeconomic Characteristics
            a. Property values, dwelling types, police information, neighborhood characteristics, occupational groups, industry, welfare data, government employment

The above list is by no means complete. The number and types of applications will continue to increase as school administrators gain more sophistication in utilizing systems concepts and computer technology to meet their existing and ever increasing need for management data.

Review of Some Existing Educational Computer Systems

To establish a more meaningful perspective of the utilization of the applications mentioned in the previous section, it is useful to briefly mention a few selected statewide and district/local users of educational computer technology. The following paragraphs are presented as brief synopses of a few statewide and district/local users of educational computer technology.

Selected Statewide Educational Computer Systems

California Educational Information System (CEIS)[49]

The CEIS, initially funded by National Defense Education Act (NDEA), Title V, Elementary Secondary Education Act (ESEA), Title III, state and local funds, was developed by the coordinated efforts of the local school districts, regional data processing/information centers and the Bureau of Systems and Data Processing in the State Department of Education. Ten, of 15 proposed, regional data processing centers are presently in operation. The system performs most of the "bread and butter" functions listed in the previous section along with an educationally orientated planning, programming budgeting system (PPBS).

Iowa Educational Information Center (IEIC)[50]

The IEIC has been under development since 1963, utilizing the resources of the University of Iowa College of Education. Funding has been from ESEA Titles IV and V, the state and local sectors. Working through a regional organization, the IEIC sets up and maintains a comprehensive system for the continuous systematic and routine collection of data about all personnel involved in the educational program and about the schools and all phases of their operation. Specifically, the IEIC has followed the recommendation of the U. S. Office of Education by establishing a total management information system based upon the five files of finance, staff, facilities, pupils and community. Iowa, though using a regional organization approach, is at the same time allowing individual districts the prerogative of developing their own system.

The IEIC, at a very early date, placed heavy emphasis upon a total information system (TIS) and with developing decision-making techniques such as PPBS, linear programming, PERT, simulation, administrative gaming and educational forecasting.

New York State Educational Information System (NYSEIS)[51]

The NYSEIS was developed under the direction of the New York State Office of Educational Finance and Management Services with the support of funds from ESEA Title III. Regional data processing has existed in New York prior to NYSEIS through 30 Boards of Cooperative Educational Services (BOCES). However, under the BOCES system of data processing, there was an enormous duplication of effort in systems analysis and programming. The NYEIS set up new data processing centers and integrated all the available information to form a total information system.

The fundamental thrust of the NYSEIS has been comprised of the classical applications of student, personnel and finance.

The Oregon Total Information System (OTIS)[52]

OTIS, initially funded by a massive ESEA Title III grant, is different from the other state systems discussed in that it is a completely centralized system using real-time remote access via teleprocessing terminals. In other words: (1) OTIS has its computer and data banks (files) located at a single facility (centralized system), (2) the participating schools access the computerized information system using devices similar to teletypewriters, or other more sophisticated equipment, (teleprocessing terminals) which may communicate over normal telephone lines (remote access) and (3) carry on two-way communications with the computer as it is actually responding to their requests (interactive real-time operation).

The OTIS system is an integrated total information system

allowing for complete cross-referencing of all files. In order to meet the many problems created by a changing and expanding information system, the OTIS staff developed a system called GEMS (Generalized Education Management System). Basically, GEMS allows participating school districts to develop an automated information system without prior data-processing experience and without hiring and training an expensive data processing staff.

Regional Data Processing -- Texas Style[53]

Regional data processing in Texas was established in 1968 with state, local and ESEA Title III funds. A total of 121 school districts participate in these services through seven regional facilities located at Houston, Fort Worth, San Antonio, Beaumont, Kilgore, Amarillo and Lubbock.

The system is organized as a TIS. Their basic applications, commonly referred to as TEXPAK, include the following: staff accounting, payroll, grade reporting, attendance accounting, property accounting, scheduling and test scoring. The basic objectives of the system are: (1) to provide computer services to help perform administrative tasks (listed above), (2) to provide a computer network for implementation of a statewide Educational Management Information System (EMIS) and (3) to provide a regional computer facility with terminals to allow for interactive real-time usage.

Selected District/Local Educational Computer Systems

Computerized School Information System (CSIS) of the Cincinnati Public Schools, Ohio[54]

The Cincinnati Public Schools, Cincinnati, Ohio, received an ESEA Title III grant in 1970 for the purpose of developing and implementing a Computerized School Information System (CSIS) for the school district of 102 schools.

The primary focus of this system is to deal with and serve as an information foundation to the educational program dimension and not to support the maintenance (e.g., budget, salary, scheduling, etc.) dimensions connected with the educational setting. The system is endeavoring to delineate information needs, gather and analyze data to meet these needs and to generate and report information to decision makers for planning and controlling the educational change process at the school unit level. The CSIS is helping in identifying, analyzing and quantifying the relationships between all inputs going into a school and educational outcomes. The information to accomplish the above is obtained from the following CSIS generated reports:

1. Exceptional Characteristics

   Quick identification of major strengths and weaknesses and

guideline for goal development or needs assessment.

2. Variable Printout

   Basic data on school's inputs and outputs (demographic and achievement data on students).

3. Student Survey

   Assessment of student attitudes as measured by a 30 item questionnaire administered to all sixth, ninth and twelfth graders.

4. Teacher Survey

   Assessment of teacher attitudes as measured by a 50 item questionnaire taken by all teachers. The results are used to offer a direction for change.

5. Parent Survey

   Assessment of parent sentiments as measured by a 22 item questionnaire.

6. Goal Survey

   Used to determine amount of agreement parents, students and teachers have regarding need areas of the school.

7. Achievement Forecast

   Evaluation of a school's success in terms of its resources by a graphical comparison of a school's predicted achievement and the school's actual achievement in reading and mathematics.

8. Trend Report

   Attempt to predict future utilizing trends represented by data accumulated over a five year period.

The system has been an excellent mechanism for goal setting, problem identification and needs analysis. It has also proved to be valuable for determining the congruence between outcomes and objectives while at the same time serving as a vital support mechanism for both an educational accountability subsystem as well as a planning-programming-budgeting-system.

Dallas Independent School District (DISD): Planning Management Information System (PMIS)[55]

The DISD is utilizing computer technology to perform the traditional applications e.g., finance, student scheduling, etc., and also in a sophisticated manner to assist in the decision-making process. The subsystem used to assist in the decision making process is known as the Planning Management Information System (PMIS). Three of the components of PMIS, which appear to have value for most administrators of a large school system, are presented below as examples of effective and efficient utilization of computer technology.

1. Personnel Simulation Model (PERSIM)

    PERSIM utilizes Markov chains[56] to simulate the flow of teachers into, through and out of the school district. Its purpose is to provide a method for making the following decisions/evaluations:

    a. Forecast the status of the faculty flow system X number of years into the future. The stature can be described in terms of such variables as races, sex, teaching assignment, college preparation and degree level.
    b. Anticipate the hiring requirements for X number of years into the future by using the same variables as in "a" above.
    c. Forecast salary costs for the school district for X number of years into the future. The effect of varying pay structures within the districts can also be accommodated.
    d. Predict the effect of a set of policy and/or environmental changes upon the faculty flow for X number of years into the future. These effects will be measured in terms of cost levels and number of teachers within the desired selected categories.

2. Selection Hierarchy Optimization Tool (SHOT) Model

    SHOT is a linear programming model that is able to compute a series of optimum "mixes" of programs or projects. Each optimum set of projects maximize student performance within a district's budgeting and policy limitations. The optimum set of projects is designed to illuminate important questions concerning strategies planning:

    a. Where am I spending my dollars now?
    b. Are my dollars being spent on measurable accomplishments?
    c. How deficient are elementary students in reading skills?
    d. How many children are presently involved in special projects?
    e. How many teachers are being used in special projects?
    f. How much does it cost to conduct projects X, Y and Z?

g. Is project X more effective than project Y?
h. Does project X cost more than project Y?
i. If project X is more effective and less expensive than project Y, why are we involved in project Y at all?
j. What would happen if we got rid of projects Y and Z and expanded project X to N more schools?
k. What if we expanded project X district-wide?

SHOT results will provide planners with a large pool of information, which when tempered by human judgment, should aid educational decision makers as they perform their complicated and difficult tasks.

3. Budget Estimation Model (BEST)

BEST enables secondary school principals to rapidly construct school schedules, estimate teacher requirements and prepare annual operating budgets.

Minneapolis-St. Paul, Minnesota: Total Information for Education System (TIES)[57]

TIES is a computerized data processing system for 29 school districts (approximately 245 thousand students in 280 schools) in the Minneapolis - St. Paul region of Minnesota. The system, which became operational in 1969, is a true TIS with a comprehensive and integrated data base.

TIES is set up with its central processing unit (CPU) located in Roseville, Minnesota. Along with receiving the usual hardcopy (printed on paper) computer printouts, all school districts have terminals and cathode ray tube (CRT) i.e., similar to a television screen, input and display units linked on line (actually wired to the computer -- in this case over telephone lines) to the CPU at Roseville. This set up allows each participating school district to interact on a real-time basis to change or produce information to help guide the education process.

Some of the data available through the TIES system are: (1) storing census records to determine school district requirements for staff, facilities and buildings, (2) student demographic data and school records, (3) personnel files, (4) payroll and finance files and (5) administrative records.

Oakland Schools (Pontiac, Michigan): Remotely Accessible Management System (RAMS)[58]

The Oakland Schools Intermediate School District for Administration serves as a central computer facility for 28 local school districts with a total of approximately a quarter million school children.

RAMS is composed of over 100 computer programs which perform the traditional applications mentioned earlier e.g., finance, personnel and pupils. The local districts communicate with the CPU over telephone lines utilizing a variety of hardware devices such as: touch-tone telephones, teletypes, IBM typewriters, IBM 1130 computers, IBM System 3 computers, Remcom 2780 terminals, etc. A significant feature of the direct access remote capability of RAMS is that the school systems' files are accessible five days a week, 24 hours a day from the local district terminal. Perhaps the most significant feature is that the local school district with rather inexpensive equipment can realize the benefits of a sophisticated and costly computerized educational management information system.

Sierra Vista Public Schools, Arizona[59]

Sierra Vista, Arizona, is a town of approximately 18000 population with a K-12 school enrollment of 4,626 in three elementary schools, one junior high school and one high school. Before installing its own computer, the school system contracted outside agencies with computer systems to do their grade reporting and class scheduling.

In August, 1972, the district installed its own system -- a Digital Equipment Corporation (DEC) PDP-8/(E) minicomputer. Since the school district was too small to afford a full-time programming and operations staff, student employees were utilized under a co-op study program. The members of the district administrative staff prepare computer-application specifications, design input and output record formats (decide what the data going in will look like and how they want the reports coming out to look) and specify the processing that is to take place.

Within the first year, the students had completed the following administrative programs: (1) student activity fund accounting, (2) budgetary and budget performance accounting, classification of budget items, the encumbrance of requests and issuance of vouchers from which the county superintendent's office issues warrants, (3) development of a district payroll system and (4) implementation of a complete attendance reporting and class scheduling program from a package provided by DEC. This total effort has been accomplished after school hours and during the summer because when school is in session, the computer is completely dedicated to instructional programs.

Trenton, New Jersey: System for Trenton's Educational Planning (STEP)[60]

In 1970, persons from both the Trenton Public Schools and from the community which it serves, expressed a need for a comprehensive systems planning instrument for making policy decisions and allocating resources. A task force was formed to analyze the need and develop a proposal. It was decided that the final system would provide the Board and Executive Staff with the ability to:

1. Test the educational impact of various allocations of resources to continuing and new projects

2. Develop plans that are directly related to educational activities

3. Translate the plans into budgets, strongly supported by realistic estimates of the probable educational impact

4. Plan far enough into the future (five years) to achieve the program continuity needed to cope successfully with the educational problems of the district.

Government Studies and Systems, Inc. (GSS) was employed as the system design group on a three year guaranteed performance agreement, wherein in each of the three years of the project, a portion of GSS payment was contingent on the delivery of specific system components.

The STEP system as it finally evolved is a set of procedures for strategic planning which relates what is spent to what is accomplished, resource inputs to educational outputs. The following is an outline of the annual cycle for STEP.

I. Major elements

   A. Annual Assessment (Update)

      1. Assessment of current educational costs and benefits, and updating all files for operating the computerized elements in the planning system. The assessment is a collection of current facts and current ratios used to generate forecasts of the future.

   B. Base Case Plan (Reference Projection)

      1. After running assessment data through the system's forecasting procedures, a five-year forecast of the school district's costs and benefits is generated.

      2. The base case answers the question: What would probably happen over the next five years if we make no changes in our current plans? The answer to that question is the basis for determining change.

   C. Policy Statement (Goals/Priorities)

      1. The desired levels of school district effec-

tiveness are reviewed. New objectives, priorities and constraints are set or those previously developed are approved (utilizes a community opinionnaire survey).

D. Project Design (Changes to Base Case)

1. Community groups participate in this phase which is intended to close the gaps between the expected levels of effectiveness in the base case and the desired levels.

E. Simulation of Alternatives

1. Specifying different costs, levels of output and revenue requirements, various combinations of new projects are run through the computerized forecasting model to generate alternative plans.

2. Alternative plans are considered, and the most cost-beneficial plan for achieving the district's objectives is recommended for implementation.

F. Approved Plan and Budget

1. Whichever plan is approved by the Board of Education becomes the approved plan.

2. If the policy deliberation required no changes, then the base case becomes the final plan.

3. At this point, the detailed budget proposal for the first year of the plan is generated.

The developers of STEP, after their initial utilization of the system concluded: (1) the system posed serious data burden on district staff even though it does not require any data which, in a well-managed school district, should not be collected anyway, (2) an output-oriented planning system is threatening to many schoolmen and boardmen since "truth in spending" is a politically sensitive matter, (3) that several of the computer software packages from STEP could be adapted to most school district's needs and (4) that the current crisis in confidence in school decision-making and budgeting demands a system like STEP.

Summary

Some of the educational computer systems that we have looked at are using their computerized data systems to assist in the decision-making process. However, as Robin C. Smith concluded in <u>The AEDS Large School Survey</u>, the emphasis is primarily placed on the "bread and butter" applications of financial accounting and personnel. In order to avoid making the computer a slave to any particular function, the top administrator of the computerized information system should be a combination systems analyst and computerized electronic data processing professional. Moreover, he should be placed on the organization chart so that he reports directly to the superintendent of schools to insure that all segments of the school system will be served equally and in an integrated manner.

Properly placed on the organization chart and with professional leadership, a computerized management information system can be constructed to meet the following objectives:

1. To keep track of individual students, staff members, programs, facilities and funds;

2. To measure what has been done in the past in order to improve, on a continuing basis, the effectiveness of future planning and action;

3. To contain an urgency index as a base in assessing various needs of students;

4. To maintain an up-to-date account of available resources to meet current needs;

5. To explain and assess the feasibility of alternative resource allocation plans;

6. To be sensitive to needed change in programs when measurements, trends or opinion so indicate;

7. To contain a feedback system to serve the administration in its efforts to optimize its planning and action;

8. To enable the needs of students to be quantified; and

9. To contain a built-in evaluation mechanism.[61]

Moreover, a true MIS (whether or not it is totally integrated) to assist school administrators in the decision-making process should utilize some computerized decision-science techniques such as: program evaluation and review technique (PERT); planning-programming-budgeting system (PPBS); simulation; linear programming; projection; and cost-benefit analysis. The extent to which any of the above are incorporated should be a function of enabling the school system to realize the ultimate objective of an information system -- "to provide data required for prudent decisions when and where demanded and with the least amount of delay."[62]

It appears that educational organizations have legitimized

utilizing computer technology on the basis of showing immediate success. This has been accomplished, both in terms of time saved and potential savings in clerical staff, by the implementation of financial applications (payroll, accounts payable, budgets/ appropriations, general accounting, etc.) and pupil applications (scheduling, attendance, grade reporting, etc.) as the main, and usually the only, components of the system. Even if both applications were completely successful, to confine the computer to such clerical tasks is to restrict the potential for effective and efficient utilization of computer technology in the administration of educational organizations.

FOOTNOTES--CHAPTER II

[1] Bumsted, A. R., *The Concept of Systems Management in Educational Data Processing*, p. 5.

[2] Smith, R. C., *The AEDS Large School System Survey. Report of Findings*, p. 4.

[3] Bumsted, op. cit., p. 5.

[4] *Ibid.*, p. 8.

[5] *EDP and the School Administrator*, pp. 2-3.

[6] *Ibid.*, p. 3.

[7] Smith, op. cit., p. 3.

[8] *EDP and the School Administrator*, p. 30.

[9] Haga, Enoch, editor, *Automated Educational Systems*, p. 16.

[10] Handy, H. W., et al., *The Computer in Education*, p. 30.

[11] Haga, op. cit., p. 17.

[12] Oettinger, A. G., *Run, Computer, Run*, p. 53.

[13] *Webster's New Collegiate Dictionary*, p. 863.

[14] *Webster's New Collegiate Dictionary*, p. 1184.

[15] Sippl, C. J., *Computer Dictionary and Handbook*, p. 312.

[16] *EDP and the School Administrator*, p. 69.

[17] Kershaw, J. A., and McKean, R. N., *Systems Analysis and Education*, p. 2.

[18] Corrigan, R. E., and Kaufman, R. A., *A System Approach for Solving Educational Problems*, p. 5.

[19] Pilecki, F. J., "The Systems Perspective and Leadership in the Educational Organization," p. 50.

[20] Oettinger, op. cit., p. 53.

[21] Pilecki, op. cit., p. 51.

[22] *New York Times*, editorial page.

[23] Sippl, op. cit., p. 17.

[24] Oettinger, op. cit., p. 55.

[25] Silvern, L. C., "Training Educational Administrators in Anasynthesis," p. 9.

[26] Oettinger, op. cit., p. 54.

[27] In computerese i.e., computer jargon, the phrase "converting it to summaries" would be replaced by the expression -- "data reduction."

[28] Grossman, Alvin, and Howe, R. L., *Data Processing for Educators*, p. 3.

[29] Van Dusseldorp, Ralph, "Some Principles for the Development of Management Information Systems," p. 32.

[30] Gothe, M. W., "The Administration of Management Information Systems in Higher Education," p. 130.

[31] Bumsted, A. R., *The Concept of Systems Management in Educational Data Processing*, p. 2.

[32] Foley, W. J., and Harr, G. G., *Management Information System Project*, pp. 8-9.

[33] *Ibid.*, p. 2.

[34] *Planning Design for Basic Educational Data System*, p. 3.

[35] Foley, op. cit., p. 10.

[36] It is a very good idea to maintain at least one duplicate set of files and that these be stored at an entirely different physical location than in the building that houses the data processing center.

[37] *Planning Design for Basic Educational Data System*. pp. 3-4.

[38] Haga, op. cit., p. 5.

[39] *EDP and the School Administrator*, p. 21.

[40] Beard, Eugene, "Computer Justified Decisions in Education," p. 33.

[41] Foley, op. cit., p. 2.

[42] Mathews, W. M., "Computer Applications in Decision-Making in Educational Administration," p. 1.

⁴³Ibid., p. 2.

⁴⁴Mize, J. H., and Cox, G. J., *Essentials of Simulation*, p. 1.

⁴⁵Mathews, op. cit., p. 2.

⁴⁶Ibid., p. 2.

⁴⁷Bumsted, op. cit., p. 12.

⁴⁸See Appendix C for the names of school systems which are using some or all of these applications.

⁴⁹Adams, Herb, "CEIS in California Regional Centers," *Journal of Educational Data Processing*, pp. 182-187.

⁵⁰Kloberdanz, Monte, "Educational Data Processing in Transition: The Iowa Educational Information Center," *Journal of Educational Data Processing*, pp. 173-180.

⁵¹Lesser, R. C., "Regional Data Processing in New York State: The New York State Educational Information System," *Journal of Educational Data Processing*, pp. 166-172.

⁵²Bennett, L. M., "OTIS: The Oregon Total Information System," *Journal of Educational Data Processing*, pp. 157-165.

⁵³Offerman, D. H., "Regional Data Processing -- Texas Style: Progress, Plans, Problems," *Journal of Educational Data Processing*, pp. 149-156.

⁵⁴Barbadora, B. M., "A Brief Description of the School Information System of the Cincinnati Public Schools," ERIC ED 079864, pp. 4-2 through 5-7.

⁵⁵"Council of the Great City Schools, Planning Management Information System," ERIC ED 079864, pp. 4-2 through 5-7.

⁵⁶A discrete random guess process in which the probabilities of occurrence of various future states depends only on the present state of the system or on the immediately preceding state and not on the path by which the present state was achieved.

⁵⁷Bovill, G. A., "Computer Project TIES in All Aspects of Education," *Visual Education*, p. 41.

⁵⁸Wood, Rex, "Remotely Accessible Management System (RAMS)," ERIC ED 087447, pp. 1-3.

⁵⁹Peltier, Barney, "Small Computer Delivers Big Improvements," *School Management*, pp. 17-18.

⁶⁰Weiss, E. H., and Ackerman, Jerry, "System for Trenton's Educational Planning (STEP): A Computer-Based Approach to Real-

izing Community Goals," ERIC ED 087443, pp. 1-16.

⁶¹Beard, op. cit., p. 34.

⁶²EDP and the School Administrator, p. 5.

CHAPTER 3

DETERMINING THE FEASIBILITY OF UTILIZING
COMPUTER TECHNOLOGY

Introduction

The demands placed upon school administrators for educational information are continually increasing. Legislators and the people in the community want to know what is going on in our schools. The educational administrator must have valid and reliable data in order to make accurate and judicious decisions in assessing and updating the educational process.[1] Facing these problems, school administrators may become so intrigued with the possibility of utilizing computer technology that they put immediate use of it for routine clerical applications ahead of an efficiently planned and integrated use of it as a total management information system.

Too many educators do not seem to understand that to develop an effective computerized data processing system requires time and a joint effort on the part of educators and computer technology specialists.[2] Educators must also be aware of the fact that all educational organizations, regardless of their many similarities, usually have quite different functional characteristics i.e., they more often than not perform or report the same activities/functions in varying ways. The implication is that it is not likely that a computer management system can be simply "plugged in" without prior planning and be expected to provide meaningful data. The educator must realize[3] that the establishment of an effective and efficient electronic data processing (EDP) system requires planning and preparation on the part of the educator combined with technical assistance from computer professionals.[4]

School administrators who do not carry out the necessary planning for effective and efficient utilization of computer technology, may find themselves with reams of meaningless computer printouts[5] and with an expensive electronic junkpile.

In-House Study or Outside Consultant

Robin C. Smith found that public school systems appear to be characterized by a "do-it-yourself" syndrome of utilizing in-house personnel in all phases of development of administrative computer systems. He also blamed this "in-house only" tendency to be a contributing factor to the apparent slow advancement of the educational computerized information systems community when compared to private industry.[6]

The criteria which can be used to determine whether or not outside consultants are required can basically be reduced to the question; are the required expertise and experience currently on the payroll?[7] Keep in mind, however, that the expertise and experience must be in all of the following areas: (1) performing a needs assessment to determine goals and objectives, (2) analysis of the organizational structure, (3) using the goals and objectives to determine the feasibility of utilizing computer technology, (4) organizing an operational computer facility staff, (5) preparing proposal requests for computer hardware and software and being able to analyze the returns, and (6) being able to plan and implement a computerized management information system. It would probably be the exception rather than the rule that any school corporation not presently involved in computerized data processing would have all of the above expertise presently on their staff. However, if some of it is present, then consultants would only be needed in the areas where expertise does not exist.

Some of the services typically offered by most computer consulting firms are:[8]

1. Management Oriented Services

    a. Needs assessment
    b. Feasibility study
    c. Organization and organizational planning
    d. MIS development
    e. Financial planning and budgetary management
    f. Management science and operations research

2. Technical Services

    a. Preparation of request for proposal (REP)
    b. Evaluation and ranking of bids
    c. Computer system design and evaluation
    d. System engineering and logic design
    e. Personnel training
    f. Materials management
    g. Product design and evaluation

3. Integrated Services

    a. Redefinition of business and corporate strategies
    b. Conversion management
    c. Installation management
    d. Quality control on material provided by vendor

In most cases, educational institutions considering the possibility of joining the age of computers will need at least some of these services performed by a consulting firm. The complexity of problems and the time required to solve them with the almost always inadequate experience level of its own staff would necessitate using an outside consultant. However, one should be extremely careful in selecting the appropriate consulting firm.

These firms have fees which range from five hundred dollars up to and over one million dollars.[9]

Totaro has proposed the following checklists to use when considering to hire a consultant firm.[10]

Areas of Investigation	Company A	Company B	Company C
Company History			
Personnel Backgrounds			
Financial Status			
Cooperativeness			
Inventiveness			
Satisfied Clients			
"Repeat" Business			
Pertinent Experience			
Fee Arrangements			

Checklist for Investigating Prospective Consultants

The decision as to how to conduct the studies necessary to determine the feasibility of utilizing computer technology i.e., using in-house staff only, using outside consultants only or using a combination of in-house staff and outside consultants, should be made carefully. This phase of the project can, if a computer system is eventually installed, have an immense affect upon its success or failure.

Determining Data Processing Needs, Goals and Objectives

An analysis of a school district's data processing needs, goals and objectives is an activity that should be performed periodically to help maintain and improve the administrative and educative processes. This type of system analysis of a school district would involve searching out all situations where the handling and use of data, relative to the districts operations, could be improved either manually or by computer technology.[11]

Specific Areas To Be Checked	Company A	Company B	Company C

Quality of Work:
   complete
   effective
   timely			

Devised Solutions:
   appropriate
   practical
   economical			

Assigned Personnel:
   competent
   objective
   responsible			

Relationships with Internal Staff:
   cooperative
   constructive			

Effectiveness of Project Managers			
Summary Evaluation of Work			
Attitude Toward Future Re-Hiring			

Checklist for Checking References of Prior Clients

The need to determine if a computer is required and if so what it would do has been stated by Swanson and Impara as:

> Although the needs of the organization may require a computer-dependent system, it is quite possible to create a system which is not built around a computer. The computer is a tool or an aid in improving and expanding the information system. When considering the development of an information system, the management of the organization should not be concerned with whether or not a computer is available, but management may come to realize the need for a computer as it describes its information requirements. It is important to bear in mind that the computer is not the information system. The computer is simply a link in the information process. The principle that an information system must serve the people (or the organization) using the system is basic: the system must reflect the needs of the user. It is obvious that if the user has a requirement, then the system should satisfy it.[12]

The AASA Committee on Electronic Data Processing (EDP) recommended, in 1967, the systems approach as a basic step to be taken before school districts move into EDP. The Committee suggested the following relative to the systems approach:

1. Systems analysis should be used as an approach to defining the information and related needs of the school system. The analysis should answer the following questions:

    a. Who is responsible for what reports?
    b. Where does the information originate?
    c. How is the gathered information treated?
    d. What resources are available to accomplish the tasks?
    e. What is done with the information processed?
    f. What are the unmet information needs?

2. Broad participation is imperative. Instructional specialist and business specialist should be involved to specify their unique informational needs and problems to be solved. The coordination of these needs should be done by the superintendent or his designated representative.[13]

The scope of a task of this nature precludes the possibility of the study being performed by a single individual. An analysis of this sort should be performed by a committee composed of administrative staff who represent each of the principal functions of the organization.[14] It may be advisable to utilize the expertise of consultants on a part-time basis. However, the understanding of the basic data requirements and flow of information within an educational organization is usually best understood by educational administrators.

The use of these personnel should result in a more realistic assessment of the present and future data processing needs of the school corporation. Documenting and analyzing the existing information system can be accomplished by: (1) describing the events which lead to data processing, (2) obtaining samples of all the input, output and file documents, (3) describing the use of information and processing by each person who handles documents, (4) charting the flow of information and documents within the organization and (5) by completely describing all files.[15] Discovering the information and data processing needs that are not satisfied by the present system requires that all users of information be interviewed to find out what data/information they need which they do not presently have. It should be explained to those interviewed that there are four basic reasons for information being needed: (1) to provide instructions for current action, (2) to provide a basis for later action, (3) to assist in answering decision inquiries and (4) to assist in answering information inquiries.[16] Unfortunately, many people do not know what they need or can use in the way of data/information to assist them in their work. This lack of user awareness is one of the major reasons that a study of this sort should be performed by people who understand the processes and requirements of the organization being studied. The analysis being performed would be enhanced if either a member of the administrative staff on the study group possessed some degree of technical competence in electronic data processing or if an electronic data processing consultant were hired to assist with this phase of the study. Along with conferring with members of the professional and nonprofessional staff and outside consultants, it may also be desirable for the committee to confer with and visit local industries and their school systems that are users of electronic data processing.

Organizational Analysis

Either by deliberate planning or through a process of evolution, most organizations are designed, to differing degrees of efficiency, to meet the requirements of the job to be done. Using manual methods, the parts of an organization responsible for data processing are organized on a decentralized basis with each department being responsible for a certain portion of the work. The processing is accomplished by passing batches of work from one section to another under an elaborate system of management, control and duplication to compensate for the poor accuracy of manual data processing.[17]

The introduction of computer technology into the organization means that most, if not all, of the data processing will be performed at a centralized location. This implies the need for an analysis and subsequent restructuring of the organization to allow for a more efficient utilization, or reduction, of the personnel previously involved in the various phases of the manual data processing system. A meaningful set of actions which must be considered when incorporating computer technology is: (1) staff reorganization and relocations, (2) realignment of communications and information flow, (3) redistribution of responsibilities and functions and (4) reallocation of staff resources.[18] Ferreting out who uses what information for what purposes and correctly integrating these people into the new system will provide for a smoother transition from a manual system to the effective utilization of a computerized system.

The organizational analysis must be performed so that inadequately and/or inefficiently organized practices, within the administrative house, can be set in order to allow for the maximum advantage of electronic data processing to be obtained.[19] Clearly then, the key to success for such an endeavor is a total commitment to the project by all echelons of the administrative staff.

Feasibility Study

Usually the initial procedures and criteria

for determination of suitability, capability and compatability of computer systems to various firms or organizations. A preliminary systems analysis of potential costs savings and new higher level of operations and decision-making; problem-solving capacity as a result of computer procurement. A study in which a projection of how a proposed system might operate in a particular organization is made to provide the basis for a decision to change the existing system.[20]

A systems study examining the job to be done, the organizational setting at the job, the information required to do it, the roles of people and various alternative ways of accomplishing the desired objectives.[21]

Each of the previous sections of this chapter are, in light of the above definitions, actually an integral part of a feasibility study. There is no unique or specific format to follow for conducting, or reporting the results of, a feasibility study. Basically though, the report should contain: (1) a comprehensive unambiguous statement of the information flow/data processing objectives, (2) a thorough analysis of the present system of information flow/data processing, (3) an analysis of present and projected future problems, (4) the cost of the manual operation and the projected cost of an automated operation, (5) a complete cost-benefit analysis in terms of personnel, software, hardware, facilities, etc., and (6) an itemization and evaluation of the advantages and disadvantages of utilizing computerized electronic data processing.[22]

The phase of the study which attempts to define how the manual operations would be computerized and at what cost, usually requires the assistance of an outside computer technology consultant. Practical experience and the literature strongly recommend that if only one consultant is used, he should not be a computer manufacturer's representative. Obviously, even though they are quite competent with regard to the application of computer technology to your situation, they nevertheless will structure their advice and recommendations in terms of their products. Following only their technical advice can result in your obtaining too much equipment, too little equipment or the wrong equipment. Even worse, you may restructure your entire organization, without regard to its present state of efficiency, to suit the hardware requirements of a particular company. Reorganization should not take place simply to allow for the compatibility necessary to interface (form a common boundary) with the equipment of a particular company. Handy was quite explicit about the use of consultants when he stated, "each (consultant) should be connected with enterprises other than those commercially engaged in the manufacture or sale of goods and services pertaining to data processing."[23]

The restriction against using a manufacturer's representative (computer sales engineer) as an outside consultant for the feasibility study is only true if but one company is used. In other words, if several companies were invited to participate in the study the findings of each, when combined, might very well offer enough alternatives to allow for a reasonable needs assessment to be made. Moreover, the services of these men, depending upon the depth of their involvement in the study, may very well be obtained free of charge. A great deal of meaningful information and assistance can be obtained from a computer company when they anticipate a potential lucrative sale.

As for independent outside consultants, there is no problem in hiring such an individual. Reputable consulting firms with no computer hardware/software or other data processing wares to sell, are located in most every major city in the country. There is another source from which expert advice on computer technology might be obtained -- a concerned citizen within the school district. It would not be uncommon to find a competent computer systems analyst residing in the school district who would be more than willing, and sometimes overanxious, to donate his services and become a member of the school corporation's feasibility study team.

The system analysis procedure for conducting a feasibility study is an accepted technique in industry but has not been readily utilized in the field of education.[24] This is rather unfortunate in that research supports the idea that systematic planning is necessary for the efficient introduction and implementation of computer technology.

Beckstrom, in a study of the organization of electronic data processing in school districts, showed that to have an efficient and successful operation, careful comprehensive planning of objectives and needs is necessary prior to installing any electronic data processing equipment.[25] In another study, Hardenbrook, in identifying processes of innovation in selected schools in Santa Barbara County, California, showed that use of a precisely defined, well-sequenced pattern of development definitely had a positive effect upon the acceptance and survival of the innovation.[26]

Pros and Cons of Computerization

The advantages of utilizing computer technology in educational administration are represented by the results obtained by effectively performing the functions delineated in Chapter II. These results, aside from being compiled with a savings in time and manpower, provide the educational administrator, faced with various decision-making responsibilities, with more relevant information and in a more meaningful form than he has previously been able to obtain.

A good many, if not most, of the problems that computers cause are usually the result of insufficient/improper planning, poor organizational structure, inadequate staffing and improper hardware configuration (having the wrong type or too much/too little equipment). Some organizations, both public and private, have pulled out their electronic computers after paying large sums of money in rent plus installation and programming (instructing the computer how to do the work) costs. The reasons they gave were: (1) installation costs were higher than expected, (2) peripheral costs continued to exceed budget limits, (3) equipment complexity caused frequent and expensive breakdowns, (4) the computer was not doing the job for which it was purchased, (5) the amount of time that everything had to be done both manually and by computer until the system had been debugged (proved to work without problems) was too long, (6) difficulty in employing qualified computer personnel, (7) computer supplier sales representatives' were too aggressive, (8) company supplied aids and training programs (when actually delivered) were too technical for the present personnel, (9) the changeover from manual systems to automated systems was not adequately planned, (10) the increased level of service cannot be properly cost accounted within the present strict budget and (11) the initial successes were shallow and few.[27]

The above reasons for decomputerization all represent factors that should have been examined, in depth, during the study phase when a determination of the feasibility of utilizing computer technology was being made. Potential users of computer technology must realize that only under proper conditions can a suitably equipped computer system handle, with little difficulty, large volumes of data generated in school administrative affairs and do so in a relatively short period of time. Some of the conditions upon which successful utilization of computers is contingent are: (1) having sufficient funds to purchase a "suitably equipped" computer system, (2) complete understanding of both the problems and the techniques to be used in solving them, (3) clearly defined and available data as input information, (4) that it be economically feasible to perform the job via computer rather than manual systems and (5) knowing what the projected workloads will be. All of the above should be ascertained during the planning phase.

The problem is that many of the dangers applicable to educational data processing that are not noticed before installation of equipment, become real problems and/or legitimate arguments against using computer technology in education. Ellis listed four such dangers:

1. Legitimacy.

    There is a tendency to permit the automation of a procedure to elevate that procedure to a level which renders us uncritical of it.

2. Overoptimism.

    It is easy to assume that computers are universally

applicable to education. However, an understanding of the limitations of computers leads to better understanding of how they can be used effectively.

3. Ad hoc Implementation.

   This danger is centered around automation in which a school develops systems which are not well enough integrated to use the output from one as input for another.

4. Using equipment designed primarily for business purposes.

   An administrator may be buying a way of doing business quite different from what he likes.[28]

The evidence seems to imply that the cons or disadvantages of computerization in education are functions of how they are utilized by the educational administrator and his staff. This same point was made in a rather clever article, "Computers - QA's Saint or Satan," by Leferre. He contends "that computers can be either good or bad -- depending upon how they are used. If we use them properly, they can be like a Patron Saint, if we use them improperly, they can smother us under tons of fire, brimstone, and paper."[29]

Summary

Determining the feasibility of utilizing computer technology is not a simple task. This chapter has attempted to give the educational administrator an awareness of how to approach the problem of examining his school system to determine whether or not it would be administratively advantageous and cost-effective to implement a computerized electronic data processing system.

A few of the more significant points discussed were: (1) an in-depth study of the information and data processing needs of a school system must have the full support of the superintendent if it is to succeed, (2) a study committee, acting under authority delegated by the superintendent, should be formed with a representation of administrators from each functional area of administration, (3) outside computer consultants should be retained if there is no in-house technical expertise available, (4) present information and data processing needs should be completely identified by: (a) following all paper around and through the present system, (b) conducting numerous interviews, (c) taking samples of all reports, records, etc., (d) charting the names, frequency and purpose of all the people who use reports, records, etc., to determine how they are used and (e) noting the shortcomings of existing methods report generation and handling with regard to speed, capacity, capability and accuracy, (5) future information and data processing needs should be projected by formulating the goals and objectives of the organization and (6) wherever possible costs should be associated with the present information and data processing procedures.

One of the expectations of a feasibility study is to arrive at answers to the following questions: (1) what is the job to be done, (2) what information is needed to do the job, (3) how can this information be obtained, processed, stored and presented, (4) what is the present information system, (5) what are the identifiable costs, (6) what are the identifiable transition problems, (7) what are the projected workloads and (8) what are the actual intermediate and long range goals, and the strategies for meeting them?[30]

Finding answers to the above questions can quite often lead to finding ways of improving the existing manual information and data processing system. This is an extremely important aspect of any feasibility study. It is of prime importance because the study is initiated to determine whether or not it is feasible to use computer technology to improve the administrative processes. The implication being that the fact that something can be done by computer does not always mean that it should be done by computer. The end result of the feasibility study might be a vastly improved manual system or it might be a decision to utilize the advantages of an educational computerized data processing system. In either case, the feasibility study, if properly conducted, is itself one more valuable tool for the educational administrator to use in improving the quality of the overall process of education.

FOOTNOTES--CHAPTER III

[1] "Planning Design for Basic Educational Data System," ERIC ED 034296, p. 5.

[2] Tidwell, Kenneth W., "The Evolving Data Processing Culture," *AEDS Journal*, p. 12.

[3] A great deal of the blame for this lack of "realization" on the part of educators can be attributed to the lack of sufficient information from computer companies.

[4] Bushnell, D. D., *The Computer in American Education*, p. 11.

[5] This problem is known in computerese (computer jargon) as "GIGO" i.e., garbage in garbage out.

[6] Smith, R. C., *The AEDS Large School System Survey. Report of Findings*, p. 3.

[7] Totaro, J. B., "How to Get Your Money's Worth with Consultants," *Data Processing Magazine*, p. 19.

[8] Sippl, C. J., *Computer Dictionary and Handbook*, p. 433 and Totaro, J. B., op. cit., p. 18.

[9] Sippl, op. cit., p. 433.

[10] Totaro, op. cit., pp. 19-20.

[11] Bushnell, op. cit., p. 11.

[12] Swanson, J. R., and Impara, J. C., "A Basis for Establishing an Information System in Education," Florida State Department of Education, p. 13.

[13] *EDP and the School Administrator*, pp. 21-23.

[14] Davis, G. B., *An Introduction to Electronic Computers*, p. 467.

[15] *Ibid.*, p. 468.

[16] *Ibid.*, p. 468.

[17] Martin, E. W., Jr., *Electronic Data Processing*, p. 479.

[18] Davis, R. M., "Techniques of Information System Design," Procedures at the first Congress on the Information Systems Serv-

ices, p. 2.

[19] EDP and the School Administrator, p. 7.

[20] Sippl, op. cit., p. 125.

[21] A Feasibility Study of a Central Computer Facility for an Educational System, pp. 2-3.

[22] Sippl, op. cit., pp. 441-443.

[23] Handy, H. W., The Computer in Education, p. 25.

[24] Bushnell, op. cit., p. 11.

[25] Beckstrom, R. S., A Plan for Organization of Electronic Data Processing in a School District, p. 80.

[26] Hardenbrook, R. F., Identification of Processes of Innovation in Selected Schools in Santa Barbara County, p. 111.

[27] Sippl, op. cit., p. 439.

[28] Ellis, Allan, "The Advantages and Disadvantages of Regionalized Data Processing in Education," Selected Proceedings Workshop #3, pp. 84-85.

[29] Leferre, H. L., "Computers - QA's Saint or Satan?" The Journal of Data Education, p. 82.

[30] A Feasibility Study of a Central Computer Facility for an Educational System, ERIC ED 027731, pp. 3-5.

CHAPTER 4

PROCEDURES FOR GETTING INTO THE COMPUTER AGE

Introduction

"'First-Time Government DP User Easy Mark for Vendors' -- There is apparently a growing trend among computer makers to prey on the inexperience of lay people in municipal governments in selling systems."[1]

The above statement refers to some of the problems that have been, and are being, experienced by both municipal governments and school corporations in the acquisition and utilization of computer hardware and software. What is happening is not so much that computer companies are "preying" on these potential customers, but rather that the customers have little or no understanding of computer technology. The result is that they frequently attempt to utilize computer hardware and/or software that is not compatible with either their needs or their pocketbooks.

The previous chapters were designed to create an awareness of the necessity of determining the school corporation's information/data processing needs and of the existing applications of computer technology which might be used to satisfy those needs. Although knowing the school corporation's information/data processing needs is a significant step along the route to utilizing computer technology, it is by no means a guarantee of successful utilization. Some of the problems that administrators face in between these two points i.e., identification of needs and successful utilization of computer technology, are quite similar to those that arise during a school building project. In both cases, the administrator must identify the school's needs (educational and technical specifications), relate these needs in an explicit manner (request for proposal-RFP) to potential vendors (computer companies, architects, contractors, etc.), evaluate the specifications submitted, select the best proposal and determine the most appropriate manner in which to finance the project.

The present chapter will deal with each of the above phases as they relate to the successful implementation of a computerized data processing system.

Organizing the Computer Facility Team

The electronic data processing (EDP) manager, as we have already noted, should be the principal advisor and report directly to the superintendent of schools on all matters pertaining to computer technology. The degree of success that will eventually be realized from the utilization of computer technology is directly related to the competence of the EDP administrator. He is the key person and should be employed very early in the initial planning stages. His technical knowledge will be invaluable in planning the computer system. This planning includes: determining the general role and function of the computer in the school system, planning the physical facilities, selecting the equipment and organizing the computer center along with helping to select and train the computer center staff. It is because of these responsibilities that it is recommended that the EDP administrator be employed as early as possible in the planning phase of the project. In selecting the administrator, however, the superintendent should look for a man who is first an educator, familiar with school administration and management problems and their solution, and secondly, a computer scientist.[2]

The following list of questions might be used to help evaluate an EDP manager that you may be considering to head up your computer installation.

1. Are routine operations going smoothly?

2. Do staff people get what they expect, about when they expect it?

3. Does the superintendent get good management reports on how data processing is progressing?

4. Is the superintendent advised of potential problems?

5. Are teachers and administrators gaining insight and getting training to use EDP as a tool?

6. Are new systems and procedures being carefully developed with the full cooperation of the people who will be in charge of them and using them?

7. Does the EDP manager know what new things data processing might be doing, and what it will take for him to implement them?

8. Will he accept outside help gracefully when it is needed?

9. Can he tell what is needed and does he know how to get it?

10. Is everything documented that should be so that a EDP manager could take over quickly, or a staff person could recognize something wrong with a seldom performed operation?[3]

The above list is not meant to be inclusive, but rather to present an idea of some of the things to consider when reviewing the EDP experience and qualifications of candidates for the position of manager of your computer installation. However, the one thing that has unanimous agreement throughout the literature is the absolute necessity of hiring an EDP manager as far in advance of acquiring computer hardware, or even of planning the scope of the facility, as possible.

There are certain jobs/tasks which must be performed in order to run a successful computer facility regardless of its physical size (amount of hardware) or scope of operation. However, the staffing requirements to accomplish these necessary jobs/tasks will be a function of the physical size and/or the scope of services to be offered -- each of which is in turn, to differing degrees, a function of the available funds. In some computer facilities, it would be necessary to have several people each of which would have the same job description whereas in other facilities, due to either size or lack of funds, there might be one person (wearing many different hats) who would perform the functions of several different job descriptions. Ideally each job should be performed by a separate and highly qualified individual. But, if circumstances i.e., money, so dictate, certain combinations of jobs may be handled -- with varying levels of adequacy -- by the same person.

Specifically, the jobs/tasks, alluded to in the above comments, and their descriptions are:

Director of Data Processing (EDP Manager)

The Director of Data Processing serves as the principal advisor to the superintendent on all matters pertaining to computer technology. It shall be his responsibility to:

1. Serve as advisor to the superintendent and staff on matters pertaining to data processing and information.

2. Develop, operate and constantly seek to improve an integrated system that will meet the needs for information and data processing and analysis services pertaining to (a) pupils; (b) personnel; (c) money, materials and facilities; (d) and the application of computer technology to curriculum and instruction.

3. Provide a system of reporting, routinely and on request, specified information needed for instructional, administrative, planning and public relations purposes.

4. Provide data processing services that will minimize clerical work, especially at the school level.

5. Provide overall coordination of the school information system with all other departments of the school system.

6. Seek constantly new applications of data processing that will improve the services and/or efficiency of the school system.

7. Evaluate educational, managerial and administrative operating systems; plan and recommend systems designed to improve the operational efficiency of the school system.

8. Provide effective leadership in recruiting, training and retaining a data processing staff of adequate size and superior quality.

9. Develop and maintain a forms control program.

10. Design and operate, in cooperation with other departments, an in-service training program for using an integrated information system.

11. Provide liaison with local, state and federal educational and governmental units to maximize the compatibility of the school district's data processing system with data processing systems of other units and to provide appropriate information required at higher educational and governmental levels.

12. Furnish the Superintendent and Board of Education with reports on the progress and needs of the Office of the Director of Data Processing.[4]

Systems Analyst

Charged with responsibility to investigate, analyze and evaluate EDP problem areas as requested; designs procedures for computer processing; and implements procedures in a computer teleprocessing environment. General responsibilities include:

1. Functioning as project leader on design and implementation of specific systems. Prepares charts, tables and diagrams to assist in analyzing problems.

2. Assisting in coordination of overall systems efforts with other project leaders and with management. Analyzes existing systems logic difficulties and suggests revisions necessary.

3. Evaluating new equipment and advising manage-

ment as to its potential. Has command of scientific and mathematical analysis.

4. Advising the district constituency on data processing benefits and capabilities.

5. Design and coordination of computer programs with the programmers on a project. Prepares computer block diagrams and may assist in flow charting.

6. Preparing presentations and holding training sessions for users concerning projects under his responsibility.

7. Suggesting to management any subjects which need further investigation or development for the schools' benefit.

8. Educating himself and co-workers in new developments and using techniques to improve the department's capability.

9. Being competent to work at the highest level in all technical phases of systems analysis.[5]

Programming Manager

Originates systems and programming assignments for the personnel responsible to him, remains knowledgeable of these assignments and their status, and trains or obtains training for programming personnel as required. Reviews and evaluates work of staff and prepares periodic performance reports. Plans, organizes and controls preparation of computer programs for the system's computer installation. Is in full charge of all programming activities. Establishes standards for block diagraming, flow charting and programming. May write and debug complex programs. Reporting responsibility is to the data processing director.[6]

Programmer

Designs and writes computer programs based on specifications outlined by the systems analyst, competent in most phases of programming and requires only general direction. General responsibilities include:

1. Flow charting specific problems for the computer

2. Designing and coding computer programs

3. Preparing program test data

4. Checking out programs for correct operation by acutal test

5. Preparing computer operator run manuals

6. Giving technical assistance to programmers at lower levels.[7]

Junior Programmer

Codes and documents EDP projects in a programming language and tests written programs. Training in operations is assumed. Works under direct supervision of programmer or manager of programming. Competent to work on several phases of programming. Assists in preparing test data, testing and debugging programs. Has detail block diagram and machine logic flow chart capabilities and the potential to aid in systems development. May evaluate and modify existing programs to incorporate changes in system requirements or equipment configurations.[8]

Manager of Computer Operations

Plans, organizes and controls the computer operations section in the operation of the computer and peripheral data processing equipment. Usually considered as being in full charge of all activities of equipment operations. Establishes detailed schedules for the utilization of all equipment in the computer operations section to obtain maximum usage. Assigns personnel to the various operations and instructs them, where necessary, so they are trained to perform assigned duties in accordance with established methods and procedures. Collaborates with personnel in other data processing sections to coordinate activities. Reviews equipment logs and reports to the manager of data processing on equipment-operation efficiency for the section.[9]

Computer Operator

Runs and has responsibility for the production of accurate and satisfactory computer and other electronic data processing output. Should be capable of setting up and operating all of the EDP equipment. Responsible for maintaining adequate inventory of computer cards, computer paper, etc. ..., for the facility.[10]

Key Punch Supervisor

Responsible to the manager of computer operations for the successful preparation of entry data coming into the system from the key punch and unit record[11] areas. Plans, schedules, supervises and directs key punching and verifying[12] activities. Assigns equitable work loads. Establishes satisfactory performance levels and supervises performance of key punch operations.[13]

Key Punch Operator

Prepares entry data in card mode or test answer sheet mode. Work must be performed within adequate accuracy levels and satisfactory time limits. Works supervised and reports to the key punch supervisor.[14]

Organizing the computer facility team by filling the above positions, or combining certain positions into a single position, should be the responsibility of the EDP manager. Aside from being the person who will be directly in charge of the staff of the computer facility, the EDP manager is, more than likely, the only administrator capable of properly interpreting the job specifications and also of knowing what level of competency would be required if certain positions had to be handled by one person e.g., hiring one person as a systems analyst/programmer instead of a systems analyst, a programmer and a junior programmer.

The typical pattern of organization that is used by computer facilities to achieve maximum efficiency and effectiveness consists of three main components: (1) research, planning and development, (2) systems design and programming, and (3) data processing and operations. The computer center for the Montgomery County Public Schools in Maryland is a successful facility which is organized according to the above system. They have formerly delineated the functions of three divisions of educational management information systems as follows:

Research, Planning and Development

This division provides liaison between the Office of Educational and Managerial Information and Analysis and the individual schools, departments and offices to develop or modify procedures pertaining to collecting, analyzing, reporting, disseminating and using information and processing data. Specifically, the functions of this division include the following:

1. Determine the feasibility of proposals and requests for information and data processing serv-

ices, estimate cost, determine priority and schedule the development and implementation of approved projects.

2. Work with other departments as projects requiring data processing services are identified to determine the user's specifications and recommend the scope of the work in relation to the total needs of the school system and future plans.

3. Provide detailed specifications and requirements for all approved projects for use in developing machine-oriented systems and computer programs.

4. Work with other departments to develop desirable applications of computer technology in all phases of school operation and in the instruction of pupils and training of staff.

5. Maintain current information on the use of computer technology in instruction.

6. Facilitate all noncomputer-oriented systems and information handling in the schools and central office.

Systems Design and Programming

This division is responsible for developing and maintaining the procedures and related computer programs required in the information system. Staff in this division will work with the Division of Research, Planning and Development to implement the desired educational data processing applications and the Division of Data Processing and Operations to assure operational efficiency. The specific functions of this division will be to:

1. Determine all outputs required to meet systems objectives including ingredients, formats, frequency and distribution.

2. Design necessary systems, forms and computer programs to implement approved projects.

3. Lay out file ingredients and formats and determine type of equipment required to handle each file.

4. Schedule receipt of all input data necessary to the work of the division.

5. Review systems with programmers and establish phasing schedules.

6. Develop or review materials to be used for program testing.

7. Perform all programming, program testing and program documentation for new applications.

8. Assist in the preparation of user manuals and materials.

9. Establish standards for all systems and programming documentation.

10. Supervise the pilot application of the system.

Data Processing and Operations

This division has the general function of collecting, processing and reporting information employing the procedures and programs developed by the Division of Systems Design and Programming. The specific functions include the following:

1. Provide assistance to users in systems operation and data utilization.

2. Maintain and control the program library.

3. Maintain and control data bank information.

4. Schedule the receipt and maintain control of all input data.

5. Edit all input and output data.

6. Maintain proper inventory levels of blank forms, cards, tapes, disks and other supplies.

7. Establish long range and short range operations plans and adjust for daily operating problems.

8. Arrange contracts for outside data recording services.

9. Control and review hardware utilization.

10. Arrange for all machine maintenance.[15]

The job descriptions and organizational pattern presented in this section are quite representative of those found both in the literature and in actual practice. They should be thoroughly understood, modified and formally structured to fit the needs of the individual computer center well in advance of actually organizing the computer facility and its team of specialists.

Developing the RFP

The RFP (request for proposal) is the school corporation's vehicle of communication between themselves and the computer companies. It is a "blueprint" by which the educational data processing needs and requirements are described to prospective bidders. In essence, it is quite similar to a set of educational specifications which would be prepared as the bidding document for a school construction project.

There can be many different formats for the RFP. However, it should contain at least the following elements:

1. A statement of the types of functions expected of the system.

2. A statement of required vendor support functions.

3. A proposal format.

4. Summary forms to be filled in by the vendor. Forms should be detailed enough to provide sufficient information for hardware and software selection. Most importantly, let the vendor extract the pertinent data from his sales literature.

5. Policy matters, evaluation techniques and standards should be available to vendors.

6. Terms and conditions.

7. Expected time frame for contract award and debriefing should also be stated.

8. A firm date beyond which rebids will not be accepted.[16]

The forms provided in the RFP to obtain technical and cost information from the vendors are extremely important. They will allow for a comparison of item costs to be made between various bidders. Moreover, the forms will also show very clearly whether or not a company uses "bundled" pricing. Lindenmeyer contends that he is better able to judge cost when all components are "unbundled" i.e., costs for hardware, software, field engineering, maintenance, etc., are all separate. Whether costs are bundled or unbundled, it is quite imperative to have the amount and type of field support that comes with the initial contract spelled out in detail.

Some other factors that should be included in the RFP are: (1) a requirement for the vendor to give reference accounts who are presently using computer systems similar, if not identical, in configuration to that proposed for your installation and who have similar system requirements,[17] (2) a requirement for successful running of "benchmark" i.e., a demonstration that the computer programs being proposed to do the school corporation's anticipated workload can in fact satisfy the school's requirements[18] and (3) detailed plans for conversion and also for future expansion.

Appendix H contains two RFP's as examples of how the document might be prepared. A cursory reading of these RFP's will point out the necessity of having the services of a technically qualified person (hopefully the EDP manager) to both prepare the document and also to help interpret the proposals which it is soliciting.

Service Bureau, In-House, Time-Sharing or Consortium

Service bureau, in-house, time-sharing or consortium all represent approaches that may be taken to realize the advantages of utilizing computer technology. The particular approach, or combination of approaches, taken usually depends upon the needs and/or available funds of the school corporation.

In order to discuss some of the advantages and disadvantages of each of the above methods, the following brief but concise working definitions are necessary: (1) service bureau - a company which either owns, leases or has access to an electronic computer and provides computer services on its own premises to the general public for a predetermined fee,[19] (2) in-house - having a self-dependent computer system for the school corporation located in one of the corporation's facilities, (3) time-sharing - a computer technique in which numerous terminal devices located in one or more school corporations can utilize a central computer concurrently for input, processing and output functions[20] and (4) consortium - an agreement or union whereby several school corporations pool their resources to jointly acquire a computer system to be housed in a facility of one of the member corporations but to be used by all of the school corporations involved. From the above definitions we can see that belonging to a consortium is somewhat similar to either using a service bureau or to time-sharing for the member corporations except the one that has the computer system in-house.

The proponents of obtaining the advantages of computerization through service bureaus use the following justifications: (1) purchasing your own computer equipment is too costly, (2) there is a problem in finding the adequate space and environmental conditions for a computer installation, (3) it is difficult and expensive to employ a competent staff, (4) the low proportion of available computer time needed to perform the required applications makes the unutilized time very expensive, (5) difficulties are found in keeping up with the changes in equipment and in methods and (6) the ability to obtain all the advantages of EDP without employing any computer specialists.[21] The major disadvantages of using a service bureau are the turn-around time i.e., the amount of time elapsed between pick-up of input and delivery of output, the rigidity of the form of the input which makes school corporation unique variations either impossible or an additional expense, having to pay extra for each application being performed and the lack of the flexibility to experiment with new applications or to utilize the full potential of computerized decision-science techniques.

All of the disadvantages of using a service bureau become some of the advantages of acquiring an in-house computer system. The only advantage of a service bureau that might be a disadvantage of a properly planned for and organized in-house system might be the overall cost of the letter.

Time-sharing can result in a savings in both equipment and personnel while at the same time providing almost all of the services of an in-house system. The extent to which time-sharing satisfies the user's needs is usually a function of the size and application capability of the system being hooked into. However, if the time-sharing school has competent personnel and has also been allotted sufficient storage space in the main computer, it could then use the system almost as though it were in-house.

The consortium approach towards utilizing computers, if carefully planned, will allow smaller school districts to realize all the hardware and software benefits of a large in-house system.[22] This implies that: (1) the main computer is of sufficient size to adequately service all of the consortium members, (2) the professional/technical staff responsible for the design, implementation and operation of hardware and software are highly competent and innovative people and (3) that a time-sharing rather than a service bureau approach is used by the participating members.

Evaluation and Selection of Hardware

Having solicited proposals for a computer system via the RFP, the educational administrator is now faced with the need to select the appropriate hardware to meet present and anticipated data processing demands within a finite budget allocation.[23] There are probably as many techniques of evaluating proposed computer systems as there are computer systems that have eventually been purchased. In other words, there is no one method of evaluation that has proven to be applicable to all situations. About the only physical factor that reaches near concensus is that the computer obtained be at least a third generation model. The generation of a computer is determined by the technology employed in the central processing unit (CPU) and in the memory hardware e.g., first generation uses vacuum tubes, second generation uses transistors and third generation uses integrated circuits.[24]

Before beginning the task of assessing computer equipment it is necessary to summarize what data are available to be used in the evaluation process. Miller, after studying various techniques from both the industrial and governmental sectors, decided that the following major data classifications would be most useful: (1) cost data, (2) performance data, (3) hardware characteristics, (4) software support and (5) miscellaneous data.[25] Reading the following complete list of items under each major heading, written in as non-technical a manner as possible, will more than likely reinforce the need, previously stated, to have a competent EDP manager available to help interpret the incoming bids.

Cost Data

1. Total cost.
2. Individual component costs.
3. Estimated cost to perform each benchmark job based on fixed hourly charge.
4. Maintenance costs.
5. Software costs (development, purchase, lease).
6. Educational and training costs.
7. Reprogramming costs (application programs).
8. Other discernible cost factors (transportation, installation, remodeling, buy-back, etc...).

Performance Data

1. Compilation time, by compiler, on benchmark tasks.
2. Linkload or collector time, by compiler, on benchmark tasks.
3. Execution time, by compiler, on benchmark tasks.
4. Time needed to initiate operating system.
5. Sort timings (from sequential and random access files).
6. Readability of printed output.
7. Number and kind of machine malfunctions.
8. Average number of machine instructions generated per line of coding by each compiler.
9. Response latency to demand processing as a function of the number of active terminals.
10. Percent of CPU utilized during benchmark.
11. Proportion of "overhead" time out of total processing time not accounted for during benchmarking.
12. Convenience of operation.
13. Compatability of existing programs (number of instructions added, deleted or changed).
14. Average number of job control parameters needed.

Hardware Characteristics

1. Full memory cycle time with and without interleaving.

2. Average machine instruction time.
3. Channel speed (total and per channel).
4. Total storage -- fast memory.
5. Total storage -- slow memory.
6. Total storage -- random access.
7. Average access speed -- random access storage for data.
8. Average access speed -- random access to operating system modules.
9. Total memory available to single user program.
10. Floating point and decimal arithmetic hardware.
11. Character coding.
12. Word size.
13. Multiprocessing capability.
14. Multiprogramming capability or batch jobs.
15. Time sharing and demand processing capability.
16. Add, subtract, multiply and divide time in single and double precision for floating point and fixed point arithmetic machine instructions.
17. Real time and time of day clocks availability.
18. Expandability of memory.
19. Virtual memory capability.
20. Total number of channels available to high speed devices.
21. Total number of remote terminals capable of support with a response delay of less than three seconds.
22. Compatibility to coding other than internal coding.
23. Maximum size of directly addressable memory.
24. Maximum tape transport transfer rate.
25. Maximum transfer rate from card reader.
26. Maximum lines per minute (132 character lines) for line printer.
27. Total storage per disk pack, if packs available.
28. Compatibility to smaller or larger machine models.
29. Total power requirement.
30. Total cubic feet of air conditioning needed and BTU dissipated.
31. Total floor space (square feet) required.
32. Memory protect features.

Software Support

1. Language availability and features.
2. Maintenance support and costs.
3. Application programs.
4. Conversion assistance.
5. Utility programs available and their features.
6. Memory utilized by operating system.
7. Memory and file protect options.
8. Levels of priority permitted.
9. Machine utilization accounting routines provided.
10. Inter language compatibility (e.g., ability to write FORTRAN subroutines in COBOL using a Common data area).

11. Debugging facilities of each language.
12. Automatic restart (recovery) procedures available.
13. File management and identification procedures.
14. Capability of system to continue processing when system components fail.
15. Ease with which operating systems are generated.

Miscellaneous Data

1. Delay before system may be delivered.
2. Proximity to other systems available for backup support.
3. Compatibility to other agencies providing a receiving date to or from the bid system.
4. Reputation of the vendor for technical and maintenance support.
5. Availability of personnel trained on the system.
6. Training programs offered by the vendor.
7. Cost and quality of supportive technical manuals.
8. Availability of equipment from other manufacturers which interface to the bid system without modification.
9. Availability of software developed by independent software houses for the bid system.
10. Expandability of the total system and potential for use in systems with faster processors.
11. Mean time between failure (MTBF) for each system component.
12. Purchase options, long term lease arrangements, guaranteed pricing for anticipated life and other cost benefits.

The above lists do not exhaust all possible relevant considerations. Most vendors have system features unique to their equipment which cannot be evaluated on all bids.[26]

Most school administrators would need the assistance of a competent computer specialist to interpret the meaning and significance of many of the hardware characteristics. However, as long as qualified professional assistance is available to evaluate the hardware so that the best suited equipment is obtained, the school administrator can still effectively and efficiently utilize computer technology without becoming a hardware expert.

Aside from not using a computer professional to assist in the hardware selection process, there are other errors made in evaluating both the suppliers and the hardware. Scharf has delineated the following:

Typical errors in evaluating suppliers

1. Tendency to consider only one manufacturer seriously.

2. Tendency to look at what a manufacturer offers

you, not what he has to offer.

3. Failure to define your own needs clearly and in sufficient detail for the manufacturer.

4. Lack of real will to cooperate with other potential partners in the fields of machine use, application, development and specialized staff.

5. Tendency to grossly underestimate costs.

6. Failure to evaluate the manufacturer as he really is and will be in your special situation as opposed to his general "reputation".

7. Lack of will to make extensive and systematically searching first hand contacts in order to evaluate user experience with corresponding machines and manufacturers.

8. Lack of relevant experience on the part of those participating in the data processing selection decision, especially as opposed to the manufacturer team which is both trained and experienced in this particular situation.

9. Failure to recognize that your own personnel may bring irrational thinking into the evaluation for personal reasons.

10. Failure to recognize that the manufacturer and certain of your own personnel will have the same vested interest in empire building.

11. Failure to analyze the half truths served by data processing salesmen.

12. Lack of will on the part of the manufacturer to really learn about you as a customer because he won't spend the time to find out what is really the situation.

13. Tendency of the manufacturer sales teams to be specialized, in spite of the fact that your organization may need interdisciplinary knowledge.

14. Failure to realize that the data processing salesman has extremely strong short-term motivation and weak long-term motivation.

Typical errors in evaluating hardware

1. Failure to go into depth regarding forms of parallel operations.

2. Failure to run actual tests.

3. Failure to take into account the effect of software organization and selection on hardware performance.

4. Failure to find out if the hardware is presently supported, sufficiently supported or supported under a particular software system so that it can be utilized without "do it yourself" software support.

5. Failure to calculate the marginal utility of adding certain hardware.

6. Failure to evaluate hardware costs in terms of other alternatives: "value analysis".

7. Tendency to evaluate in terms of old myths.

8. Failure to design an efficient system before calculating needed hardware capacity.

9. Failure to anticipate Parkinson's Law: the tendency of users to expand needs so as to fill the capacity of a new EDP facility within unexpectedly short time.

10. Tendency to confuse traditional needs simply because we have been unable to satisfy real needs economically before.

11. Failure to give serious consideration to independent peripheral suppliers, thus forcing yourself to take the economic consequences of the package deal even on the hardware side.[27]

Armed with the ready assistance of his computer specialist to interpret and evaluate the technical hardware specifications along with being cognizant of the above typical errors in evaluating suppliers and hardware, the school administrator will be able to approach the process of evaluating and selecting hardware in an intelligent and meaningful manner.

Evaluation and Selection of Software

In his computer dictionary, Sippl defines software as:

> The internal programs or routines professionally prepared to simplify programming and computer operations. These routines permit the programmer to use his own language (English) or mathematics (Algebra) in communicating with the computer. Various programming aids that are frequently supplied by

the manufacturers to facilitate the purchaser's efficient operation of the equipment. Such software items include various assemblers, generators, subroutine libraries, compilers, operating systems and industry -- application programs. Most types of programs in the computer software library are offered in several versions to run in systems configurations of different sizes and compositions.[28]

During the 1960's it used to be that hardly anyone (especially educators) considered any software that wasn't generated in-house or supplied "free" by the computer manufacturer. But users are now recognizing that software costs money and that "freebees", in most cases, aren't part of the overall package any longer.[29] Since computer programs are not in general patentable or copyright-able, the computer companies protect their software on the basis of the "trade secret" law. This law defines a trade secret broadly as "any formula, pattern, device or compilation of information which is used in one's business, and which gives him an opportunity to obtain an advantage over competitors who do not know or use it."[30] The computer companies have implemented the trade secret protection for their computer programs through a License-to-Use. This license can specify either that the use is for a specified period of time or that the use is forever. For the first case the financial arrangement is usually a monthly fee and a paid-up or full-payment lease in the second case.[31]

Contrary to popular opinion, just because a computer company has a particular software application package, does not necessarily imply that the package: (1) is completely debugged (will run without errors), (2) will satisfy your requirements or (3) will be written in a language capable of being run on your equipment configuration. Fortunately, most proprietary software is warranted. This means that the seller has the responsibility to fix whatever bugs may be noticed during the warranty period.[32]

Another factor to consider is that more often than not, the company supplied software package must be modified to suit the particular user's needs. If, in this case, the modifications will be extensive enough so that the resultant software becomes quite user unique, then the administrator should be concerned with: (1) will there be an additional charge for the modification effort, (2) is the resultant package still considered to be proprietary software or is it user owned software and (3) in either case is the software still under warranty?

The school administrator in trying to evaluate and select software should also be aware of the following typical errors in this process compiled by Scharf:

    1. Failure to run actual tests on actual machines and to ensure that the evaluation team is trained and given time to do this (benchmarking).

2. Failure to measure real performance.

3. Tendency to think in traditional ways.

4. Failure to comprehend all the complex factors which affect software performance on a given machine.

5. Failure to use experienced experts for independent software evaluation.

6. Failure to recognize and calculate the amount of man effort on your own part which is necessary in order to actually use certain software.

7. Failure to use the same standards for comparative evaluation of different manufacturers' machines.

8. Tendency to evaluate on the basis of past needs, not future needs.

9. Failure to evaluate the concept of security in software.

10. Failure to evaluate the complexity of using software efficiently on a day to day basis.

11. Failure to evaluate single software parts in terms of the effect on the total economics of the software system.[33]

The preceding discussion has been primarily concerned with selecting and evaluating software application packages. The same factors also apply to the various language processors that should be capable of being run on your computer system e.g., COBOL (COmmon Business Oriented Language), FORTRAN (FORmula TRANslation), ALGOL (ALGOrithmic Language), RPG (Report Program Generation), PL/1 (Programming Language/one), BASIC (Beginners All-purpose Symbolic Instruction Code), manufacturer unique assembly language, etc.

Financing: Purchase, Rental, Third Party Lease, Other

Purchase

If a school corporation could afford an outright purchase of a computer system, it would be the least expensive method of payment. The reduced expense is a result of not having to pay the interest that is required on a multi-year purchase agreement and also because of the savings realized from the educational discounts offered by some companies on outright purchases.[34] However, if an outright purchase is made, the equipment should be of the latest model to avoid running the risk of obsolescence.

This obsolescence may occur because of the introduction of better equipment, because the equipment will not handle the volume of work or because new systems concepts require a different kind of equipment configuration.[35] A rough rule of thumb that has been cited is that a computer installation with a useful life of more than five years should be purchased rather than rented. Although, in any specific case, the breakeven point is dependent on such factors as the number of shifts the equipment is used and the types of present and anticipated applications.[36] Even with the outright purchase method of acquiring a computer system there will still be the continual cost of a maintenance contract, which definitely should be acquired.

Rental

The major advantage of vendor rental agreements are the capability to easily arrange for an upgrade without the necessity and inconvenience of having to dispose of existing equipment, and the capability to easily arrange for the replacement of particular pieces of equipment which may be only marginally serviceable. The last advantage may be very important in cases of mechanical equipment subject to rapid wear e.g., card punches, printer, card readers, etc.[37] Other, more obvious, advantages of renting are the absence of a large capital outlay, the assumption by the manufacturer of all maintenance costs and the removal of the risk of obsolescence for the user.[38]

Though there are several different types of rental agreements, most of them: (1) charge per piece of equipment (2) charge for each special feature e.g., interpret feature on keypunches, and (3) have a base rental for X hours (usually around 176 hours) of actual use per month with an additional lower rate for all hours above that level (some manufacturers do not charge educational users for the excess hourly usage).[39]

Third Party Lease

Under this method of financing the educational institution purchases the equipment on an outright basis in order to take advantage of all potential educational discounts, resells the equipment to a third party who actually supplied the initial capital and then leases the equipment from the third party.[40] Though lease agreements vary, they typically have provisions such as:

1. User agrees to lease for a minimum period, say, five years, with purchase and trade-in options.

2. The lease payment includes maintenance and other charges.

3. There is no additional charge for second- or third-shift operations (except some additional

maintenance charges).

4. After the minimum period, the lease charges drop to a lower rate.

5. If the lease is terminated before the minimum period is up, the user must pay a termination charge.[41]

After examining third party leasing, Kaimann and Drzycimski listed the following advantages and disadvantages:

Lessee Advantages

1. The rental payment for identical hardware is 10-30% less when leasing via a lessor intermediary.

2. The minimum monthly maintenance contract from the vendor is usually paid by the lessor.

3. The user may utilize additional system time at no direct additional rental charge.

4. A flexible schedule of rental charges might be arranged at the inception of the contract.

Lessee Disadvantages

1. A longer lease is frequently required than that offered by the vendor.

2. There is a question of vendor support with respect to personnel and software assistance to the installation.

Lessor Advantages

1. Given that computer systems hardware constitutes a capital asset acquisition, an immediate investment tax credit of 7% is applicable if the duration of use spans at least an eight year period.

2. A choice of depreciation schemes is available and the appropriate technique is a function of the income of the lessor.

3. The result of advantages one and two create a highly favorable cash flow posture.

4. Assuming that the lessor is in a tax bracket higher than the maximum applicable to corporations (48% or higher) the lessor gains greater benefit through depreciation.

5. The demand for systems hardware is growing.

Lessor Disadvantages

1. The declared useful life of the capital asset must span a minimum of eight years to qualify for the full investment tax credit.

2. To make the acquisition attractive to the lessor, it would be important for the contract to take the form of a financial lease.

3. To utilize the full benefits of the contractual arrangements it is necessary that the income of the lessor causes him to reside in a high tax bracket.

4. At some point during the life span of the lease, the lessee might choose to complement the hardware configuration by requesting additional capacity in terms of more tape or disk drives or maintenance memory.

5. The lessor might have to assume personnel and software support functions if the vendor declines to do so.

6. Lessee opts to abandon the lessor by cancelling the lease or by not exercising the renewal option.[42]

Other

Most vendors offer a lease rental plan which includes an option to purchase the equipment. Though the provisions vary from vendor to vendor, they usually provide for educational discounts and low interest rates. The major advantages of vendor lease arrangements are the capability to easily arrange for upgrade without having to dispose of the existing equipment and the capability of readily arranging for the replacement of separate pieces of equipment which may be only marginally serviceable.[43]

Another method of acquiring a computer system is by forming a computer cooperative. These cooperatives usually will provide for the development of a data processing capability far beyond the financial limitations of any of the individual districts involved.[44] In most cases none of the participating districts will want to assume the cost of program development and/or operations that are not readily applicable to their own immediate requirements. The easiest way to resolve this potential problem is simply to share costs on a proportionate basis i.e., the costs of program development, hardware, personnel, etc., are shared proportionately by each participating district. On the other hand, management policies and other decisions relative to operating the facility would be made on an equal basis by all the member school districts.⁴⁵

Summary

Unfortunately, there is no "cookbook" approach for getting into the computer age. However, the phases described in this chapter should serve to create a necessary, if not sufficient, level of awareness of the steps involved in organizing, planning, evaluating, financing and implementing an administratively oriented educational computer facility.

The initial action recommended is the hiring of an administratively and technically competent EDP manager far enough in advance so that he would be able to assist in each phase of the process. Then once a total plan for all uses and applications of computer technology for the school district has been drawn up, the specifications for the system are then delineated. These "specs" are for hardware, software, support services, and benchmark testing. The RFP containing all of these specs and requests is then sent to numerous vendors to solicit their bids.

At this point it should be worth noting that the best system for your needs is not always the most expensive. However, if not, closer examination may show that for the same cost of what appears to be the best but also most expensive system, other proposed systems could be expanded to include new and attractive features thus making one of them the most cost-effective choice.⁴⁶ This is quite similar to not buying the stripped-down top-of-the-line automobile, but rather buying the next model and adding on all of the desired items so that the end result is a customized machine for the same price as the top model without all the same options.

An important point to keep in mind when reviewing the vendors' responses to your RFP is simply that "any question that might not be answered by the proposal, should be treated as being negative...all commitments and promises must be in writing."⁴⁷

Also, a complete computer facility will require other items of related equipment such as: (1) keypunching machines, card sorters, forms bursting and collating machines, special purpose storage cabinets, card files, office furniture, etc... These items should be ordered so that their delivery is either before or coincides with the time the computer is installed.⁴⁸

Finally, approaching the process of acquiring a computer system in a haphazard manner can cause the following law of Harvey Golub to become a reality:

> No major computer project is ever installed on time, within budget, with the same staff that started it, nor does the project do what it is supposed to.⁴⁹

FOOTNOTES--CHAPTER IV

[1] Lundell, E. D., Jr., "First-Time Government DP User Easy Mark for Vendors," Computerworld, p. 3.

[2] Handy, H. W., et al., The Computer in Education, p. 31.

[3] Anderson, G. E., Jr., "Questions to Consider When Rating Your EDP Manager," Nations Schools, p. 66.

[4] Handy, H. W., et al., op. cit., pp. 32-33.

[5] EDP and the School Administrator, pp. 43-44.

[6] Ibid., p. 43.

[7] Ibid., p. 43.

[8] Ibid., p. 42.

[9] Sippl, C. J., Computer Dictionary and Handbook, p. 455.

[10] EDP and the School Administrator, p. 42, and Sippl, op. cit., pp. 456-457.

[11] Machines which use punch cards or mark sense cards as input e.g., tabulating machines, card reproducers, mark sense reader/punch, collators, etc.

[12] Checking computer cards to make sure that they are properly punched.

[13] EDP and the School Administrator, op. cit., p. 43.

[14] Ibid., p. 43.

[15] Handy, et al., op. cit., pp. 57-59.

[16] Botten, L. H., Methods Used in a Recent Computer Selection Study, pp. 2-4 through 2-5.

[17] Ibid., pp. 3-8 through 3-9.

[18] Martin, B. A., "Guidelines for Contracting for Computer Related Services," Computers and Automation, p. 18.

[19] Cerullo, M. J., "Teaching About Service Bureau," Journal of Data Education, p. 7.

[20] Sippl, op. cit., p. 328.

[21]Cerullo, op. cit., p. 10.

[22]Fullum, S. J., "Use of a Time-Sharing Computer in a Regional Data Processing Center at Burlington County, New Jersey," ERIC ED087469, p. 3.

[23]Miller, W. G., "Selection Criteria for Computer System Adoption," *Educational Technology*, p. 71.

[24]Summers, J. K., and Sullivan, J. E., *The State of the Art in Information Handling*, ERIC ED051552, p. 17.

[25]Miller, op. cit., p. 72.

[26]Ibid., pp. 72-74.

[27]Scharf, T. G., "How Not to Choose an EDP System," *Datamation*, pp. 73-74.

[28]Sippl, op. cit., p. 292.

[29]Hansen, R. W., and Shostak, A. D., "How to Evaluate and Select Software," ERIC ED087460, p. 1.

[30]Frombolz, H. J., "Legal Protection of Computer Programs and Confidential Information," *Proceedings of the COMPON 73 IEEE*, p. 106.

[31]Hansen and Shostak, op. cit., p. 2.

[32]Ibid., p. 2.

[33]Scharf, op. cit., p. 74.

[34]Botten, L. H., *Methods Used in a Recent Computer Selection Study*, ERIC ED086208, p. H-1.

[35]Davis, G. B., *An Introduction to Electronic Computers*, p. 477.

[36]Ibid., p. 478.

[37]Botten, op. cit., p. H-2.

[38]Davis, op. cit.

[39]Ibid., p. 476.

[40]Botten, op. cit., p. H-1.

[41]Davis, op. cit., p. 478.

[42]Kaimann, R. A., and Drzycimski, E. F., "Third Party Leasing," *Journal of Data Management*, pp. 33-46.

[43] Botten, L. H., *Report of Computer Selection Study Committee*, ERIC ED-86207, p. 6-3.

[44] Hoffmeister, J. K., "A Locally Financed Schools Computer Cooperative," AEDS Monitor, p. 7.

[45] *Ibid.*, p. 9.

[46] Mosmann, Charles, *Academic Computers in Service*, p. 151.

[47] Roberts, E. W., *Data Processing Curriculum for Education*, p. 206.

[48] Handy, *et al.*, *op. cit.*, p. 37.

[49] Groobey, J. A., "Maximizing Return on EDP Investments," *Journal of Data Management*, p. 28.

CHAPTER 5

DISCUSSION AND CONCLUSIONS

The Role of the Computer in Educational Administration

The role of the computer in educational administration changes as more educators become more knowledgeable in its potential uses. Van Dusseldorp claims that there are four observable stages through which computerized educational information systems have moved:

1. The applications approach.
   This was used when we first began to apply the computer to the processing of educational information. Most of the applications were of a clerical nature - payroll, financial accounting, school scheduling, grade reporting, teacher certification, distribution of state aids, and the like.

2. The integrated systems approach.
   This was an attempt to integrate the information from the various applications so that information from any one area would be related to information from each of the other areas.

3. The total systems approach.
   This was an attempt at avoiding unnecessary duplication in gathering, storing and processing data for separate systems. Using this approach, all the information needed by an educational agency was identified, sources of the necessary data were located, then the data elements were gathered at the appropriate sources, stored and processed through a central system.

4. The management information system approach.
   The primary emphasis is on providing the information needed by management. The information needs of management are first determined. Then the system is built to provide the information needed by management for planning, decision-making and control.[1]

Utilizing the management information system approach, the educational administrator will have the capability of performing each of the necessary applications listed in stage one while at the same time enhancing the ability to make management decisions and therefore increasing the operational efficiency of the school district.[2] Hansen noted in no uncertain terms that "if an administrator cannot, in a matter of minutes, discover every educational project's exact status, its cost and income to date . . . then decision makers are being short changed."[3] While it usually is not necessary to perform the above in minutes, it is definitely the role of the educational computer system to: (1) provide speed in accumulation of data and accuracy of computation, (2) provide an extensive up-to-date data bank on which to base management decisions, (3) provide increased information to lessen areas of uncertainty thereby reducing the degree of managerial risk-taking and (4) to provide decision-making capability based upon previous experience.[4]

Another significant role of the computer in education is in simulation. There already are imaginative methods of utilizing the data in the information system to simulate varying courses of action from the financial and organizational areas e.g., new educational programs, new teacher salary schedules, new tax programs, new forms of organization etc. One such device called Cost Ed Model developed by Education Turnkey Systems, Inc., of Washington, D. C., is a computerized mathematical simulation of how educational decisions and patterns of school operations affect costs. It traces the contribution to total school costs of decisions on class size and instructional materials expenditures, of teachers' salaries, and of all school building design parameters. A total of over 1,800 distinct cost-influencing factors may be considered in a Cost Ed Model.[5]

Using simulation devices of this type, the educational administrator can: (1) determine how much a change in one area will affect a cost someplace else, (2) determine how much of a change is needed in one area to offset a change in another area, (3) analyze the economics each pilot program in terms of its cost and the resulting level of achievement, (4) can simulate and analyze the possibility of running a pilot project and (5) examine the key relationships among budgets, facilities, plans, schedules, staff assignments and educational results.[6] Clearly, computer techniques of this sort are actually a part of a potential PPB system.

In discussing the role of the computer in education, Johnson made the point that the computer is "not an icon" but rather "a means to an end, and if it becomes an end in itself, it is no longer a tool but rather a monster created by management."[7] He also pointed out the problem whereby computer personnel sometimes tend to view themselves as high priests of a new religion. The solution to this problem, since the computer as well as the computer personnel are there to assist the educational administrator, is simple - replace them.[8]

The computer can be one of the best friends of the administrator, but it can also create confusion, misinformation, bad feelings and deficits. Caffrey and Mossman upon examining this situation stated that "the choice is not up to the machine, nor to the technical people who run it. It is up to the administrator who evokes the educational goals of the organization and who leads those around him to achieve them. The computer only amplifies and implements decisions made or approved by the administrator."[9]

Perhaps the most significant aspect of the computer in education is the effect that it has upon management techniques and the role of the school administrator.

> The aspects of educational technology that have the greatest potential for redefining the role of the superintendent of schools are systems management theory, the revolution in information processing, and the emergence of new specializations. These related phenomena will have tremendous potential impact on the most fateful function of the administrator: decision-making. By combining the discipline of systems management with the data processing capability of the computer, it is conceivable that the decision-making process in school administration may be revolutionized. In the past, the administrator could claim that he had too little information to anticipate all possible alternative decisions. The new (existing) computer capability will (does) deprive tomorrow's (today's) administrator of this excuse.[10]

Computer Techniques as They Relate to General Management

The decision-science techniques discussed earlier e.g., PERT, PPBS, simulation, linear programming, projection, the Cost Ed Model and management information systems, represent but a few of the alternatives that should be used by administrators in order to function effectively and efficiently in the continual-change environment created by the demands of a knowledge-based society.[11]

Successful management is a combination of many factors. Utilizing computer-assisted tools such as the decision-science techniques as one of the contributing factors, management can more effectively achieve their primary purposes while at the same time realizing the following "add-on" benefits:

1. Bridging the communication gap by means of participation throughout all phases of systems development and implementation.

2. More effective planning in terms of activities to be accomplished and their interrelationships.

3. The ability to more effectively monitor and

control progress of projects.

4. The great benefit of better staff and management relations by meeting commitments expeditiously and efficiently.

5. A much better system because of better planning and monitoring.

6. Improved future project planning and control because of better planning and control presently.[12]

The necessary prerequisites for establishing an effective computer facility are in themselves general management techniques that should be adhered to regardless of the existence of a computer-assisted management system. Price has organized these prerequisites into what he refers to as "The Ten Commandments of Data Base:"

1. Identify data requirements.

2. Define file requirements.

3. Design general system.

4. Evaluate justification criteria.

5. Project planning control.

6. Data management control.

7. Develop, test and document.

8. Plan security protection.

9. Educate and implement.

10. Audit and evaluate results.[13]

The above list may or may not represent the essential elements required for conducting each and every management project. However, what is important is not the specific items but rather the process which they, as a group, represent. The simple fact of the matter is that in order to utilize computer technology in an efficient and effective manner, management must approach each problem in an organized, systematic and quite precise manner. The implication is that even without the assistance of a computer this type of an approach towards general management would most certainly lead to a more effective and efficient organization.

Everything taken into account, the most important aspect of the computer as it relates to general management is its potential to raise management's ability to make accurate decisions. The enigmas confronting the top levels of management of any complex organization are not the relatively formal problems faced by engineers and physicists. Rather they are gnarled, ill structured and contain elements of uncertainty. With respect to this situation, the editors of Fortune Magazine stated:

> The great achievement of the computer is that it is enabling the executive to clear away some of the uncertainty that surrounds him, to subtract some of the variables from the circumstances that fret him, to convert many ill-structured and inherently insoluble problems into well-structured and partly soluble ones, to rely less on hunches and intuition and more on analysis, to behave less like an artist and more like a scientist in disposing of routine matters, and to save his creativity and imagination for more important work.[14]

The contents of this work were designed to create a level of awareness amongst educational administrators relative to the potential for effective and efficient utilization of computer technology. However, before deciding to attempt the implementation of any of the procedures or techniques that have been discussed, the following quote by E. Wainright Martin, Jr., should be read very carefully.

> The electronic computer and its associated information technology present a tremendous opportunity to the organization that is prepared to use them intelligently. On the other hand, it is apparent that the use of an electronic computer is not a panacea for poor management. As a matter of fact, excellent management is required to utilize an electronic computer successfully, and the management attributes emphasized by the computer are already of great importance to management success. Thus, the use of a computer is likely to make poor management more apparent, and good management even better.[15]

Don't Re-Invent the Wheel

Public school systems invariably exhibit a tendency to "re-invent the wheel" characterized by a "do-it-yourself" syndrome in the development of administrative computer applications.[16] Whether because of: a false sense of economy; a lack of comprehension of the difficulty of designing, developing and implementing a complex computer system; or an unfounded confidence in their own computer technology capabilities most school districts use in-house staff for the development of their computer applications. The problem is not the use of in-house staff, which hopefully is highly competent, but rather that they tend to develop unique and original software packages.

Original development of computer software, in light of the availability of commercial software packages and of software packages that have already been developed/modified by school districts with similar characteristics, is an inexcusable waste of resources -- both human and financial (to say nothing of re-creating all the problems and errors i.e., "bugs," that have already been resolved). As has already been discussed, the evaluation and selection of software should be an integral part of the process of acquiring a computer system.

Whether it be for the initial phase of software acquisition and implementation or for later efforts to increase the software applications, the first step is to determine if the necessary software already exists. This can be accomplished by checking with: other school districts utilizing computer technology, computer manufacturers, computer software companies, professional magazines and journals, etc. In quite a few instances, the necessary software, which if modified to accommodate local district unique requirements, will be found already in use.

Aside from proprietary software, which a school corporation is legally bound not to share, most school districts are more than willing to provide other districts with a particular software package that they may be using. This is quite common via the many "users groups" which various educational data processors have formed specifically for the purpose of sharing information.

Before deciding upon original development of a particular software package, the wise EDP manager should always investigate to see if it already exists so that precious time and money will not be wasted in re-inventing the wheel.

Caveat Emptor

'Bad Package Cited in Delay of School Grades': Toledo, Ohio -- School districts in this area have experienced delays of up to five weeks in getting out grades, as well as spending thousands of dollars in overtime because of problems with . . . (company X) . . . software program.[17]

'First-Time Government DP User Easy Mark for Vendors': Salem, Mass. -- There is apparently a growing trend among computer makers to prey on the inexperience of lay people in municipal governments in selling systems.[18]

'DC Computer SNAFUS Force Vote Recount': Washington, D.C. -- . . . Both hardware and software malfunctions on a . . . (company Y computer) . . . combined to delay final election totals more than 22 hours after the polls closed.[19]

With computer systems as with used automobiles, let the

purchaser take care. We have already made note of the computer salesman's short-term exuberance and long-term lack of interest. However, experiencing hardware and/or software problems due to an inappropriate hardware configuration or because of a software "bug" during a regular production run, is usually the fault of the user and not the fault of the computer company. The reason for placing the onus upon the customer is simply that: (1) the computerized data processing needs of the organization should have been sufficiently determined during the planning stage to be spelled out in detail in the RFP -- computer companies will usually respond with a proposal of a configuration of equipment in excess of what is actually required and (2) most potential software problems can be determined and corrected during a properly administered benchmark run.

Though it is doubtful that any major computer company would deliberately attempt to sell a school district equipment that would not meet its needs, whose fault is it if the district does not really know its own needs? Hopefully, the information contained in this work will allow the educational administrator to avoid the embarrassment, to say nothing of the cost, of obtaining hardware and/or software that either does not meet his needs or simply does not function correctly. In any event, "buyer beware."

FOOTNOTES--CHAPTER V

[1] VanDusseldorp, Ralph, "Management Responsibility for Information Systems," *Educational Technology*, pp. 38-39.

[2] Johnson, G. R., "Computer as a Management Tool: Ten Ways to Make the Computer Serve You," *College Management*, p. 18.

[3] Hansen, Burdette, "The Computer and Management Information in Education Related Organizations," *Educational Technology*, p. 15.

[4] Gott, John, and Gengwish, Nick, "What the Public Schools Superintendent Needs to Know About Computer Hardware and Software," *AEDS Monitor*, p. 8.

[5] *The Cost-Ed Model; A New Economic Tool for the School Administrator*, Education Turnkey Systems, Inc., ERIC ED057462, p. 4.

[6] *Ibid*., pp. 5-8.

[7] Johnson, *op. cit*., p. 18.

[8] *Ibid*., p. 18.

[9] Caffrey, John, and Mossman, C. J., *Computers on Campus*, American Council on Education, p. 184.

[10] Knezevich, S. J., and Eye, G. G., *Instructional Technology and the School Administrator Final Report*, ERIC ED044789, pp. 141-142.

[11] Mathews, W. M., "Computer Applications in Decision-Making in Educational Administration," ERIC ED087436, p. 1.

[12] Rudy, H. L., *et al*., "Planning and Controlling Computer-Based Systems Development," ERIC ED087458, p. 18.

[13] Price, G. F., "The Ten Commandments of Data Base," *Journal of Data Management*, p. 35.

[14] Burck, Gilbert, and the Editors of Fortune, *The Computer Age*, Harper Torchbooks, pp. 101-102.

[15] Martin, E. W., Jr., *Electronic Data Processing An Introduction*, Richard D. Irwin, Inc., p. 533.

[16] Smith, R. C., *The AEDS Large School System Survey. Report of Findings*, ERIC ED073679, p. 3.

[17]_Computerworld_, February 13, 1974, pp. 1 and 4.

[18]_Computerworld_, March 21, 1973, p. 3.

[19]_Computerworld_, October 2, 1974, p. 1.

BIBLIOGRAPHY

Adams, Herb, "CEIS in California Regional Centers," *Journal of Educational Data Processing*, Summer, 1969.

Alspaugh, John W., "Utilization of Computing and Data Processing in Education," *Clearing House* ERIC No. EJ002370, April, 1969.

Anderson, G. Ernest, Jr., "Questions to Consider When Rating Your EDP Manager," *Nation's Schools*, December, 1969.

Anderson, Walter R., and Sonn, Edward H., "How to Select a Minicomputer," *Computers and Automation*, December, 1969.

Banach, William J., "Public Relations, Computers and Election Planning," *School Management*, October, 1971.

Banahart, Frank W., *An Automated Inventory System for Educational Physical Facilities: A Technical Report*, Florida State University, Tallahassee, Educational Systems and Planning Center, 1971, ERIC No. ED060559.

Barbadora, Bernard M., "A Brief Description of the School Information System of the Cincinnati Public Schools," Paper presented at the Association for Educational Data Systems Annual Convention, New Orleans, Louisiana, April 16 through 19, 1973, ERIC No. ED087445.

Beard, Eugene, "Computer Justified Decisions in Education," *Educational Technology*, March, 1970.

Beckstrom, Ronald S., "A Plan for Organization of Electronic Data Processing in a School District," Unpublished Ed.D. dissertation, University of Utah, 1967.

Bennett, Lowry M., "OTIS: The Oregon Total Information System," *Journal of Educational Data Processing*, Summer, 1969.

Botner, Stanley B., "Cooperative Use of ADP by Public Entities," *Journal of Data Management*, June, 1971.

Botten, LeRoy H., *Methods Used in a Recent Computer Selection Study*, Andrews University, Compution Center, Berrien Springs, Michigan, HEW, ERIC No. ED086208, February 20, 1973.

    Report of Computer Selection Study Committee, Andrews University, Computing Center, Berrien Springs, Michigan, ERIC No. ED086207, December 13, 1973.

Bovill, G. A., "Computer Project Ties In All Aspects of Education," *Visual Education*, November, 1972, ERIC No. EJ066676.

Bromberg, Howard, "Software Buying," *Datamation*, September 15, 1970.

Brooks, Frederic P., Jr., "Why Is The Software Late?" *Journal of Data Management*, August, 1971.

Brooks, Garr D., and Lyon, James M., "The Lexicon of the Computer," *Educational Technology*, April, 1972.

Bumsted, Alec R., "The Concept of Systems Management in Educational Data Processing," A Professional Paper, System Development Corporation, ERIC No. ED047353, Santa Monica, California, January 6, 1969.

Burch, Gilbert, and editors of FORTUNE, *The Computer Age*, Harper and Row, 1965.

Burns, Frederick J., "Data Systems Documentation: Why and Where," *AEDS Journal*, June, 1969.

Bushnell, Don D., *The Computer in American Education*, John Wiley and Sons, New York, 1967.

Butt, Robert E., and Guthrie, Chester L., "Can Small School Systems Use Computers?" *School Management*, August, 1972.

Caffrey, John, and Mossman, C. J., *Computers on Campus*, Washington, D.C., American Council on Education, 1967.

Campbell, Thomas C., "Total Information for Educational Systems Development," *AEDS Monitor*, October, 1970.

Castetter, William B., *The Personel Function in Educational Administration*, The Macmillan Co., 1971.

Cerullo, Michael J., "Teaching About Service Bureaus," *Journal of Data Education*, March, 1972.

College and University Business, May, 1972, ERIC No. EJ058451.

Corrigan, R. E., and Kaufman, R. A., *A System Approach for Solving Educational Problems*, Operation PEP, Office of the San Mateo County Superintendent of Schools, October, 1967.

Council of the Great City Schools, Washington, D. C., "Planning Management Information System: A Project to Develop a Data Processing System for Support of the Planning and Management Needs of Local School Districts," PMIS Project, ERIC No. ED079864, Final Report, Year 2.

Crowe, Robert L., "The Computer and Personnel Selection," *School Management*, August, 1972.

Cummins, William K., "Educational Administration for Systems Technology and Innovations," <u>AEDS Journal</u>, ERIC No. EJ062362, June, 1972.

Davis, Gordon B., <u>An Introduction to Electronic Computers</u>, McGraw-Hill, New York, 1965.

Davis, Ruth M., "Techniques of Information System Design," Maximal set of actions which must be considered in order to earn the title of Design of Information System, Procedures at the first Congress on the Information Systems Sciences, Hot Springs, Va., November, 1962.

Dorn, Phillip H., "How to Evaluate a Time-Sharing Service," <u>Datamation</u>, November, 1969.

The Dunn and Bradstreet Business Library, <u>What the Manager Should Know About the Computer</u>, revised edition, Thomas Y, Crowell Co., N. Y., 1970.

<u>EDP and the School Administrator</u>, American Association of School Administrators, 1967.

Education Turnkey Systems, Inc., <u>The Cost-Ed Model; A New Economic Tool for the School Administrator</u>, Education Turnkey Systems, Inc., ERIC No. ED057462, Washington, D. C., September, 1971.

Ellis, Alan, "The Advantages and Disadvantages of Regionalized Data Processing in Education," Selected Proceedings Workshop #3: An Introduction to Educational Data Processing, Association for Educational Systems, Washington, D. C., 1967.

<u>The Use and Misuse of Computers in Education</u>, McGraw-Hill, New York, 1974.

<u>A Feasibility Study of a Central Computer Facility for an Educational System</u>, DHEW, ERIC No. ED027731, General Learning Corp., Washington, D. C., Office of Education (DHEW), Washington, D. C., Bureau of Research, Final Report, February, 1968.

Floyd, Jerald D., <u>The Computer: An Administrative Dilemma</u>, Northern Illinois University, DeKalb, 1972, ERIC No. ED069116.

Foley, Walter J., and Harr, Gordon G., "Management Information System Project," Iowa Center for Research in School Administration, ERIC No. ED072528, University of Iowa, Iowa City, 1972.

Frombolz, H. J., "Legal Protection of Computer Programs and Confidential Information," <u>Proceedings of the COMPCON, 73 IEEE</u>, 1973.

Fullum, Stephen L., "Use of a Time-Sharing Computer in a Regional Data Processing Center at Burlington County, New Jersey," Paper presented at the Urban Regional Information Systems Association Conference, Atlantic City, New Jersey, August 31, 1973, ERIC no. ED087469.

Gilmore, Hal, and Swezey, Don, "Intermediate School District 109 Data Processing Cooperatives," AEDS Monitor, November, 1970.

Goodland, John I.; O'Toole, John F.; and Tyler, Louise L., Computers and Information Systems in Education, Harcourt, Brace and World, Inc., N. Y., 1966.

Gordon, William L., "Selecting the Proper Data Processing Equipment," AEDS Journal, December, 1968.

Gothe, Michael W., "The Administration of Management Information Systems in Higher Education," Unpublished Ed.D. dissertation, Indiana University, Bloomington, Indiana, August, 1973.

Gott, John, and Gengwish, Nick, "What the Public Schools Superintendent Needs to Know About Computer Hardware and Software," AEDS Monitor, October, 1971.

Groobey, John A., "Maximizing Return on EDP Investments," Journal of Data Management, September, 1972.

Grossman, Alvin, and Howe, Robert L., Data Processing for Educators, Educational Methods Inc., Chicago, 1965.

Gunther, Max, "Computers - Their Built-in Limitations," Playboy, October, 1967.

Haga, Enoch (ed.), Automated Educational Systems, The Business Press, Elmhurst, Ill., 1967.

Hamblin, John W., "Institutional Research Today, Systems Analysis Tomorrow," AEDS Journal, Washington, D. C., March, 1970.

Handy, H. W.; Gibbs, Helen; and Bell, John C., The Computer in Education, Educational Service Bureau, Inc., Washington, D. C., 1970.

Hansen, Burdette, "The Computer and Management Information in Education-Related Organizations," Educational Technology, August 30, 1968, ERIC No. ED043238.

Hansen, Duncan N., The Role of Computers in Education During the 70's, Florida State University, Tallahassee, Computer-Assisted Instruction Center, May 15, 1970.

Hansen, R. W., and Shostak, A. D., "How to Evaluate and Select software," Paper presented at the Association for Educational Data Systems Annual Convention, New Orleans, Louisiana, April 16 through 19, 1973, ERIC No. ED087460.

Hardenbrook, R. F., "Identification of Processes of Innovation in Selected Schools in Santa Barbara County," Unpublished Ed.D. dissertation, University of Southern California, 1967.

Hartley, Harry J., "Twelve Hurdles to Clear Before You Take On Systems Analysis," The American School Board Journal, July, 1968.

Harvey, Glenn B., "Rounding Second Base with Data Base: DePaul University's Experience," Paper presented at the Association for Educational Data Systems Annual Convention, New Orleans, Louisiana, April 16 through 19, 1973, ERIC No. ED087459.

Havemann, Ernest, "Computers - Their Scope Today," Playboy, October, 1967.

"How Schools Can Make Computers Pay Their Way," The Office, August, 1968.

Heinich, Robert, Management Models and Instructional Productivity, Indiana University, Bloomington, 1973, HEW, ERIC No. ED086205.

Johnson, Gary R., "Computer as a Management Tool: Ten Ways to Make the Computer Serve You," College Management, April, 1972.

Kalmann, Richard A., and Drzycimski, Eugene F., "Third Party Leasing," Journal of Data Management, January, 1969.

Karush, Arnold, "Performance Measurement," Journal of Data Management, July, 1971.

Kelly, John W., "Getting Started in Data Processing: The Pioneers are the Ones with the Arrows," AEDS Monitor, January, 1969.

Kenner, James B., and Retz, R. Robert, "Planning for an EDP System," School Management, October, 1970.

Kenny, John J., "Objectives for EDP Organizations," Journal of Data Management, January, 1972.

Kershaw, Joseph A., and McKean, Roland N., Systems Analysis and Education, Rand Corporation, Santa Monica, California, 1959.

Kitts, Kent D., "Creating a Data Processing Staff from Within," Journal of Data Management, October, 1968.

Kloberdanz, Monte, "Educational Data Processing in Transition: The Iowa Educational Information Center," *Journal of Educational Data Processing*, Summer, 1969.

Knezevich, Stephen J. (ed.), and Eye, Glen G. (ed.), *Instructional Technology and the School Administrator Final Report*, American Association of School Administration, ERIC No. ED044789, Washington, D. C., 1970.

Leferre, Henry L., "Computers -- QA's Saint or Satan?", *The Journal of Data Education*, December, 1970.

Lesser, Richard C., "Regional Data Processing in New York State: The New York State Educational Information System," *Journal of Educational Data Processing*, Summer, 1969.

Lewis, John F., "Mechanization Doesn't Always Pay," *The Office*, July, 1968.

Lewis, S. G., *An Information System for a District School Administrator. Operation PEP/Executive Information Systems*, ERIC No. ED051551, Mitre Corp., Bedford, Mass., June, 1970.

Lindenmeyer, Leonard R., "Computer Procurement Policy Under Unbundling," *Journal of Data Management*, October, 1970.

Link, Albert D., "The Computer and the Salary Schedule Ritual," *School Management*, December, 1971.

Louchary, John W., and Tondon, Murray (eds.), *Educational Information System Requirements: The Next Two Decades*, Papers from a conference held at the University of Oregon, Eugene, August, 1967, ERIC No. ED033399.

Lundell, E. D., Jr., "First-Time Government DP User Easy Mark for Vendors," *Computerworld*, March 21, 1973.

Martin, B. A., "Guidelines for Contracting for Computer Related Services," *Computers and Automation*, April, 1970.

Martin, E. Wainright, Jr., *Electronic Data Processing An Introduction*, Richard D. Irwin, Inc., Homewood, Ill., 1965.

Martin, James and Norman, Adrien, *The Computerized Society*, Penguin Books, Middlesex, England, 1973.

Mathews, Walter M., "Computer Applications in Decision-Making in Educational Administration," Paper presented at the Association for Educational Data Systems Annual Convention, New Orleans, Louisiana, April 16 through 19, 1973, ERIC No. ED087436.

Miller, William G., "Selection Criteria for Computer Systems Adoption," *Educational Technology*, October, 1969.

Mitchell, Edward E., "Systematic Approach to the Decision Process in Education," *AEDS Monitor*, February, 1970.

Mize, Joe H., and Cox, Grady J., *Essentials of Simulation*, Prentice-Hall, Inc., Englewood Cliffs, N. J., 1968.

Montgomery County School Board, Norristown, Pennsylvania, "Planning-Programming-Budgeting System, Intermediate Unit Planning Study, Final Report," ERIC No. ED055367, Bureau of Elementary and Secondary Education (DHEW/OE), Washington, D. C., DPSC-67-4280, September, 1971.

Morgan, Robert M., *A Review of Educational Applications of the Computer, Including Those in Instruction, Administration and Guidance*, ERIC No. ED032768, Stanford, August, 1969.

Mosmann, Charles, *Academic Computers in Service*, Jossey-Bass, San Francisco, 1973.

New York Times, New York, New York, June 16, 1967.

Oettinger, Anthony G., *Run, Computer, Run*, Collier Books, New York, N. Y., 1969.

Offerman, Donald H., "Regional Data Processing -- Texas Style: Progress, Plans, Problems," *Journal of Educational Data Processing*, Summer, 1969.

Ollivier, Robin T., "A Technique for Selecting Small Computers," *Datamation*, January, 1970.

Palmer, Leonard J., "Save 75% of Your EDP Costs," *The Office*, January, 1969.

Peltier, Barney, "Small Computer Delivers Big Improvements," *School Management*, April, 1974.

Petrie, Thomas A., "A Computer Co-op for Small School Districts," *AEDS Journal*, September, 1969.

Pilecki, Francis J., "The Systems Perspective and Leadership in the Educational Organization," *Educational Administration Quarterly*, Winter, 1970.

"Planning Design for Basic Educational Data System," South Carolina State Department of Education, Columbia, 1969, ERIC No. ED034296.

Price, Gerald F., "The Ten Commandments of Data Base," *Journal of Data Management*, May, 1972.

"Project Termination Report (PTR) School Management and Evaluation System," P. L. 89-10, Title III, Project No. 45-70-010-3, Board of Education of the City School District of the City of Cincinnati, May 4, 1973.

Roberts, Ellis W., *Data Processing Curriculum for Education*, Final Report Project No. 8-0449, U. S. Department of Health, Education, and Welfare, Harrisburg, Pa., Commonwealth Development Association, 1968.

Rudy, Harry L., et al., "Planning and Controlling Computer-Based Systems Development," Paper presented at the Association for Educational Data Systems Annual Convention, New Orleans, Louisiana, April 16 through 19, 1973, ERIC No. ED087458.

Scharf, Tom Gilb, "How Not To Choose an EDP System," *Datamation*, April, 1969.

Schwartz, Eugene S., "Computer Evaluation and Selection," *Journal of Data Management*, June, 1968.

Scotese, Peter G., "How to Pick an EDP Manager," *The Office*, December, 1970.

Silvern, Leonard C., "Training Educational Administrators in Anasynthesis," *Educational Technology*, February, 1972.

Sippl, Charles J., *Computer Dictionary and Handbook*, Howard W. Sams and Co., Inc., Indianapolis, Indiana, 1966.

Smith, Robin C., *The AEDS Large School System Survey. Report of Findings*, AEDS, ERIC No. ED073679, Washington, D. C., November, 1972.

"A Personnel System for People," AEDS paper, ERIC No. ED087450, 1973.

Sorensen, J. L., "A Solution to the Small Company's EDP Dilemma," *Journal of Data Management*, April, 1969.

Stollar, Dewey H., and Ray, John R., "A Learned Computer Acquisition," *AEDS Monitor*, March, 1971.

Summers, J. K., and Sullivan, J. E., "The State of the Art in Information Handling," Operation PEP/Executive Information Systems, ERIC No. ED051552, Mtre Corp., Bedford, Mass., June, 1970.

Swanson, James R., and Impara, Jamces C., "A Basis for Establishing an Information System in Education," Non-Technical paper Division of Research, Florida Department of Education, Tallahassee, Florida, 1968.

Tidwell, Kenneth W., "The Evolving Data Processing Culture," *AEDS Journal*, September, 1968.

Tondow, Murray, "Computers in the Schools: Palo Alto," *Datamation*, June, 1968.

"What Can Computers Do For You?" <u>School Management</u>, September, 1966.

Totaro, J. Burt, "How to Get Your Money's Worth With Consultants," <u>Data Processing Magazine</u>, April, 1970.

Van Dusseldorp, Ralph, "Management Responsibility for Information Systems," <u>Educational Technology</u>, May, 1971.

"Some Principles for the Development of Management Information Systems," <u>Management Information Systems in Higher Education: The State of the Art</u>, ed. by Charles B. Johnson and William G. Ketzenmeyer, Duke University Press, Durham, N. C., 1969.

Vretsky, Myron, "Look to Business for Answers to Campus Computing Problems," College and University Business, September, 1972.

Ward, Obie, and Poules, Cynthia, "Trends in OMR Techniques and Equipment," AEDS No. ED087461, Atlanta Public Schools, Georgia, Computer Center, 1973.

<u>Webster's New Collegiate Dictionary</u>, G. and C., Merriam Co., Springfield, Mass., 1956.

G. and C., Merriam Co., Springfield, Mass., 1973.

Weiss, Edmund H., Ackerman, Jerry, "System for Trenton's Educational Planning (STEP): A Computer-Based Approach to Realizing Community Goals," ERIC No. ED087443, New Jersey State Department of Education, Trenton, April, 1973, Paper presented at AEDS Annual Convention at New Orleans, Louisiana, April 16 through 19, 1973.

Wilsey, Carl E., "Are You Ready for Your Own Data Processing Center," <u>The Education Digest</u>, January, 1969.

Wilson, Harold B., "How the Total Information System is Designed," <u>The Office</u>, February, 1967.

Wilson, Michael J., <u>Cybernetics and Education: A Colloquium</u>, New England School Development Council, 1962.

Wiseman, Toni, "Bad Package Cited in Delay of School Grades," <u>Computerworld</u>, February 13, 1974.

Wisniewski, R. P., "Variable Programs - Get the Job Done," <u>AEDS Monitor</u>, January, 1970.

Withington, Frederic G., "Write Your Own," <u>Datamation</u>, October 1, 1970.

Wood, Rex, "Remotely Accessible Management System (RAMS)," Paper presented at the Association for Educational Data Systems

Annual Convention, New Orleans, Louisiana, April 16 through 19, 1973, ERIC No. ED087447.

Yoo, Ronald, "Contracting Effectively for Computer Software," *Journal of Data Management*, November, 1970.

Young, Robert B., "The Computer and the Contract," *Datamation*, November 1, 1971.

APPENDIX

APPENDIX A

Glossary of Related Terms

ACCESS, IMMEDIATE - Pertaining to the ability to obtain data from, or place data in, a computer storage device or register directly, usually in a relatively short period of time.

ACCESS, RANDOM - (1) The process of obtaining information from, or placing information into, a storage device where the time required for such access is independent of the location of the information most recently obtained or placed in storage. (2) Pertaining to a device in which the process of random access can be achieved without effective penalty in time.

ACCESS, TIME - The time interval between the call for, and the delivery of, information from a storage unit of the computer.

ACCUMULATOR - A part or register of a digital computer which stores the results of arithmetic operations.

ADDRESS - (1) An identification, represented by a name, label, or number, for a register or location in storage. Addresses are also a part of an instruction word along with commands, tags, and other symbols. (2) The part of an instruction which specifies an operand for the instruction.

ADDRESS CODE - Instruction codes used to locate a specific item of data within storage units of a computer.

ALGOL (algorithmic Language) - An arithmetic language by which numerical procedures may be precisely presented to a computer in a standard form. The language is intended not only as a means of directly presenting any numerical procedure to any suitable computer for which a compiler exists, but also as a means of communicating numerical procedures among individuals. The language itself is the result of international cooperation to obtain a standardized algorithmic language. The International Algebraic Language is the forerunner of ALGOL.

ALGORITHMIC - Pertaining to a constructive calculating process usually assumed to lead to the solution of a problem in a finite number of steps.

ALPHANUMERIC - A combination of characters which include letters of the alphabet, numerals, and other symbols such as punctuation or mathematical symbols.

ANALOG COMPUTER - A computer which represents variables by physical analogies; thus, any computer which solves problems by translating physical conditions such as flow, temperature, pressure, angular position, or voltage into related mechanical or electrical quantities and uses mechanical or electrical equivalent circuits as an analog for the physical phenomenon being investigated. In general, it is a computer which uses an analog for each variable and produces analogs as output. Thus an analog computer measures continuously, whereas a digital computer counts discretely.

ANALYSIS, SYSTEMS - The examination of an activity, procedure, method, technique, organization, or business to determine what must be accomplished and how the necessary operations may best be accomplished.

ANALYST - A person skilled in the definition and development of techniques for the solving of a problem, especially techniques for solutions on a computer. A person skilled in framing the alternatives in a decision-making situation.

APPLICATION - The system of problems to which a computer is applied. Reference is often made to an application as being either of the computational type, wherein arithmetic computations predominate, or of the data processing type, wherein data-handling operations predominate.

ARITHMETIC UNIT - The unit of a computer which contains the circuits for performing arithmetic operations.

ASSEMBLER - A computer program which operates on symbolic input data to produce from them machine instructions by carrying out such functions as translation of symbolic operation codes into computer operating instruction, assignment of locations in storage for successive instruction, or computation of absolute addresses from symbolic addresses. An assembler generally translates input symbolic codes into machine instructions item by item and produces as output the same number of instructions or constants which were defined in the input symbolic codes. Synonymous with assembly program and related to compiler.

AUTOMATED DATA PROCESSING (ADP) - (1) The implementation of processes by automatic means. (2) The theory, art, or technique of making a process more automatic. (3) The investigation, design, development, and application of methods of rendering processes automatic, that is, self-moving or self-controlling.

BINARY - A characteristic, property, or condition in which there are but two possible alternatives; e.g., the binary number system, in which 2 is the base and only the digits zero (0) and one (1) are used. Clarified by binary number system.

BINARY NUMBER SYSTEM - A number system which a computer can comprehend and which uses the number 2 as a base (as opposed to the decimal system which uses the number 10). Only two choices or digits are used, 0 and 1.

Decimal Number	Equivalent Binary Number Designation
0	0
1	1
2	10
3	11
4	100
5	101
6	110
7	111
8	1000
9	1001
10	1010

BIT - (1) An abbreviation of binary digit. (2) A single character in a binary number. (3) A single pulse in a group of pulses. (4) A unit of information capacity of a storage device. The capacity in bits is the logarithm to the base two of the number of possible states of the device. Related to capacity, storage.

BRANCH - The selection of one or two or more possible paths in the flow of control based on some criterion. The instructions which mechanize this concept are sometimes called branch instructions; however, the terms transfer of control and jump are more widely used.

BRANCHING - A method of selecting the next operation for the computer to execute while the program is in progress, based on the computer results.

BUFFER - (1) An internal portion of a data-processing system serving as intermediary storage between two storage or data-handling systems with different access times or formats; usually to connect an input or output device with the main or internal high-speed storage. (2) A logical OR circuit. (3) An isolating component designed to eliminate the reaction of a driven circuit on the circuits driving it; e.g., a buffer amplifier. (4) A diode.

BUG - Any mechanical, electrical, or electronic defect that interferes with computer operation, including a defect in programing. Correcting this defect is commonly called debugging.

BYTE - (1) A generic term to indicate a measurable portion of consecutive binary digits; e.g., an 8-bit or 6-bit byte. (2) A group of binary digits usually operate upon as a unit.

CAPACITY, STORAGE - The number of elementary pieces of data that can be contained in a computer storage device. Frequently defined in terms of characters in a particular code or words of a fixed size that can be so contained. Related to bit (4).

CARD CODE - A combination of punches used to represent alphabetic and numerical information in a punched card.

CARD, EIGHTY (80)-COLUMN - A punch card with 80 vertical columns representing 80 characters. Each column is divided into two sections, one with character positions labeled 0 through 9, and the other labeled 11 and 12. The 11 and 12 positions are also referred to as the X and Y zone punches, respectively. Sometimes called the Hollerith card or IBM card. Holes of rectangular shape are usually punched in this card in accordance with a specified code.

CARD, NINETY (90)-COLUMN - A punch card with 90 vertical columns representing 90 characters. The columns are divided in half horizontally, so that the vertical columns in the upper half of the card are numbered 1 through 45, and those in the lower half, 46 through 90. Six punching positions may be used in each column; these are designated, from top to bottom, to represent the digits 0, 1, 3, 5, 7, and 9 by a single punch. The digits 2, 4, 6, and 8 and other characters may be represented by a combination of two or more punches. Sometimes called the Powers card or Remington Rand card. Holes of circular shape are punched usually in this card in accordance with a specified code.

CENTER, DATA-PROCESSING - A computer installation providing data-processing service for others, sometimes called customers, on a reimbursable or nonreimbursable basis.

CENTRAL PROCESSING UNIT (CPU) - The group of components of a data-processing system which contains the logical, arithmetic, and control circuits for the basic computer system.

CHANNEL - (1) A path along which information, particularly a series of digits or characters, may flow. (2) One or more parallel tracks treated as a unit. (3) In a circulating storage, a channel is one recirculating path containing a fixed number of words stored serially by word. (4) A path for electrical communication. (5) A band of frequencies used for communication.

CHARACTER - (1) One symbol of a set of elementary symbols such as those corresponding to the keys on a typewriter. The symbols usually include the decimal digits 0 through 9, the letters A through Z, punctuation marks, operation symbols, and any other single symbols which a computer may read, store, or write. (2) The electrical, magnetic, or mechanical profile used to represent a character (1) in a computer and its various storage and peripheral devices. A character may be represented by a group of other elementary marks, such as bits or pulses.

CIRCUIT - (1) A system of conductors and related electrical elements through which electrical current flows. (2) A communications link between two or more points.

CLOCK, REAL-TIME - A clock which indicates the passage of actual time, in contrast to a fictitious time set up by the computer program, such as elapsed time in the flight of a missile, wherein a 60-second trajectory is computer in 200 actual milliseconds or a 0.1-second interval is integrated in 100 actual microseconds.

COBOL (Common Business Oriented Language) - A programing system which uses basic English language and then translates the English phrases into computer code programs which can be understood and executed by the computer.

CODE - (1) A system of symbols for meaningful communication. (2) A system of symbols for representing data or instructions in a computer or a tabulating machine. (3) To translate the program for the solution of a problem on a given computer into a sequence of machine language or pseudoinstructions and addresses acceptable to that computer. Related to encode. (4) A machine language program.

COLLATE - To take two or more sets of related information already in sequence and merge them in sequence into a single group.

COMMON LANGUAGE - Refers to a uniform language in which all information is in a form which can be interpreted by all units in a data-processing system. This language may be punched cards, paper tape, or magnetic tape. With this common language, the units of a system can "talk" to each other.

COMPARE - To check information against related information to determine whether it is identical, larger, or smaller, or whether it is in the sequence desired.

COMPATIBILITY EQUIPMENT - The characteristic of computers by which one computer may accept and process data prepared by another computer without conversion or code modification.

COMPILER - A computer program more powerful than an assembler. In addition to its translating function, which is generally the same process as that used in an assembler, it is able to replace certain items of input with series of instructions, usually called subroutines. Thus, where an assembler translates item for item and produces as output the same number of instructions or constants as were put into it, a compiler will do more than this. The program which results from compiling is a translated and expanded version of the original. Related to assembler.

CONCURRENT PROCESSING - The ability to work on more than one program at the same time.

CONFIGURATION - A group of machines which are interconnected and are programed to operate as a system.

CONSOLE - A portion of the computer which may be used to control the machine manually; correct errors; determine the status of machine circuits, registers, and counters; determine the contents of storage; and manually revise the contents of storage.

CONSTANTS - The quantities or messages which will be present in the machine and available as data for the program and which, usually, are not subject to change with time.

CONTROL UNIT - The section of the computer containing the circuits and devices which govern the overall operation of a system -- the "brains" of the system. The portion of a computer which directs the sequence of operations, interprets the coded instructions, and initiates the proper commands to the computer circuits preparatory to execution.

CONVERTER - A device which converts the representation of information, or which permits the changing of the method for data processing from one form to another; e.g., a unit which accepts information from punch cards, records the information on magnetic tape, and possibly includes editing facilities.

CYBERNETICS - The field of technology involved in the comparative study of the control and intracommunication of information-handling machines and the nervous systems of animals and man in order to understand and improve communication.

DATA - A general term used to denote any or all facts, numbers, or letters and symbols that refer to or describe an object, idea, condition, situation, or other factor. It connotes basic elements of information which can be processed or produced by a computer. Sometimes data are considered to be expressible only in numerical form, but information is not so limited.

DATA CELL - An external, large-capacity memory unit which can be placed on-line or off-line to a computer. Memory capacity starts with 400 million characters per unit and can be extended to a total of more than 6 billion.

DATA PROCESSING - A series of operations used for handling information. Data processor may be defined as any group of people and/or machines organized and acting together to perform the processing of information.

DATA REDUCTION - The computer job of bringing large masses of raw data to their simplest form and then organizing them in a useful manner.

DATAMATION - A shortened term for automatic data processing taken from data and automation.

DECISION - The computer operation of determining whether a certain relationship exists between words in storage or registers and taking alternative courses of action. This is effected by conditional jumps or equivalent techniques. Use of this term has given rise to the misnomer "magic brain"; actually the process consists of making comparisons by use of arithmetic to determine the relationship of two terms (numeric, alphabetic, or a combination of both); e.g., equal, greater than, or less than.

DECODE - (1) To apply a code so as to reverse some previous encoding. (2) To determine the meaning of individual characters or groups of characters in a message. (3) To determine the meaning of an instruction from the set of pulses which describes the instruction, commands, or operation to be performed.

DIAGRAM - (1) A schematic representation of a sequence of subroutines designed to solve a problem. (2) A coarser and less symbolic representation than a flow chart, frequently including descriptions in English words. (3) A schematic or logical drawing showing the electrical circuit or logical arrangements within a component.

DIGITAL COMPUTER - A computer which processes information represented by combinations of discrete or discontinuous data as distinguished from an analog computer for continuous data. More specifically, it is a device for performing sequences of arithmetic and logical operations not only on data but on its own program. Still more specifically, it is a stored program digital computer capable of performing sequences of internally stored instructions, as opposed to calculators, such as card-programed calculators, on which the sequence is impressed manually.

DISK, MAGNETIC - A storage device on which information is recorded on the magnetizable surface of a rotating disk. A magnetic disk storage system is an array of such devices, which are mounted on movable arms.

DRUM, MAGNETIC - A cylinder, with a surface coating of magnetic material, which stores binary information by the orientation of magnetic dipoles near or on its surface. Since the drum is rotated at a uniform rate, the information stored is available periodically as a given portion of the surface moves past one or more flux-detecting devices called heads located near the surface of the drum.

EAM (Electric Accounting Machine) - The set of conventional punch card equipment including sorters, collators, and tabulators.

ENCODE - (1) To apply a code, frequently one consisting of binary numbers, to represent individual characters or groups of characters in a message. Inverse of decode. (2) To substitute letters, numbers, or characters for other numbers, letters, or characters, usually to intentionally hide the meaning of the message except to certain individuals who know the enciphering scheme.

EOF - End of File. Termination or point of completion of a quantity of data. End-of-file marks are used to indicate this point.

EQUIPMENT, INPUT - (1) The equipment used for transferring data and instructions into an automatic data-processing system. (2) The equipment by which an operator transcribes original data and instructions into a medium that may be used in an automatic data-processing system.

EQUIPMENT, OFF-LINE - The peripheral equipment or devices not in direct communication with the central processing unit of a computer.

EQUIPMENT, ON-LINE - Descriptive of a system and of the peripheral equipment or devices in a system in which the operation of such equipment is under control of the central processing unit and in which information reflecting current activity is introduced into the data-processing system as soon as it occurs. Thus, directly in-line with the main flow of transaction processing.

EQUIPMENT, PERIPHERAL - The auxiliary machines which may be placed under the control of the central computer. Examples of this are card readers, card punches, magnetic tape feeds, and high-speed printers. Peripheral equipment may be used on-line or off-line depending upon computer design, job requirements, and economics. Clarified by equipment, off-line.

ERASE/PURGE/ZERO-OUT - To remove information from a memory unit of a computer.

EXTERNAL MEMORY - A storage unit (such as a magnetic tape, disks, or data cell) which is external to the computer but which can be connected to and controlled by the computer.

FEEDBACK - The part of a closed loop system which automatically brings back information about the condition under control.

FLOW CHART - A diagram or graphic representation of the logical flow of information in a data-processing system. A diagrammatic representation of a plan for the sequence of operations in solving a problem on a computer.

FORTRAN (Formula Translator) - A programing system developed by IBM which translates statements expressed in a format similar to algebraic equations into a computer language.

GATE - A circuit with one output and many inputs designed so that the output is activated only when certain input conditions are met.

HARDWARE - A term used to describe the mechanical, electrical, and electronic elements of a data-processing system. A general term that encompasses all physical equipment used in EDP such as the computer or central processor and peripheral gear such as key punch, tape drives, and printer.

HOLLERITH CODE - The standard 12-channel code used in some tabulating card systems.

INDICATOR - A light or other signal, generally on the console, which is used to indicate that a particular condition has occurred in the computer.

INDIRECT ADDRESSING - A method of cross-reference. A memory location which, when addressed, will tell you where to find the correct location of the fact being sought.

INFORMATION RETRIEVAL - A method of cataloging vast amounts of related data so they can be called up any time they are needed, with speed and accuracy. The recovery of desired information or data from a collection of documents or other graphic records.

INPUT-OUTPUT DEVICE - A general term for the equipment used to communicate with a computer and the data involved in the communication. Synonymous with I/O.

INPUT - (1) Information or data transferred or to be transferred from an external storage medium into the internal storage of the computer. (2) Describing the routines which direct input as defined in (1) or the devices from which such information is available to the computer. (3) The device or collective set of devices necessary for input as defined in (1).

INQUIRY - A technique whereby the interrogation of the contents of a computer's storage may be initiated at a keyboard.

INSTRUCTIONS - (1) A set of characters which defines an operation together with one or more addresses, or no address, and which, as a unit, causes the computer to perform the operation on the indicated quantities. The term instruction is preferable to the terms command and order; command is reserved for a specific portion of the instruction word, i.e., the part which specifies the operation which is to be performed; order is reserved for the ordering of the characters, implying sequence, or the order of the interpolation or differential equation. (2) The operation or command to be executed by a computer, together with associated addresses, tags, and indices.

INTERCOUPLE - To connect two machines or machine components mechanically, electrically, or electronically.

INTERFACE - A common boundary between automatic data-processing systems or parts of a single system.

INTERPRETER - (1) A punch card machine which will take a punch card with no printing on it, read the information in the punched holes, and print a translation in characters in specified rows and columns on the card. (2) An executive routine which, as the computation progresses, translates a stored program into machine code and performs the indicated operations, by means of subroutines, as they are translated. An interpreter is essentially a closed subroutine which operates successively on an indefinitely long sequence of program parameters, the pseudo-instructions and operands. It may usually be entered as a closed subroutine and left by a pseudo-code exit instruction.

I/O - The abbreviation for input/output.

ITERATIVE - Describing a procedure or process which repeatedly executes a series of operations until some condition is satisfied. An iterative procedure can be implemented by a loop in a routine.

LANGUAGE - A system for representing and communicating information or data between people or between people and machine. Such a system consists of a carefully defined set of characters and rules for combining them into larger units, such as words or expressions, and rules for word arrangement or usage to achieve specific meanings.

LANGUAGE, MACHINE-ORIENTED - (1) A language designed for interpretation and use by a machine without translation. (2) A system for expressing information which is intelligible to a specific machine; e.g., a computer or class of computers. Such a language may include instructions which define and direct machine operations and information to be recorded by or acted upon by these machine operations. (3) The set of instructions expressed in the number system basic to a computer, together with symbolic operation codes with absolute addresses, relative addresses, or symbolic addresses.

LIBRARY - (1) A collection of information available to a computer, usually on magnetic tapes. (2) A file of magnetic tapes.

LOCATION - A storage position in the main internal storage which can store one computer word and is usually identified by an address.

LOGIC - (1) The science dealing with the criteria or formal principles of reasoning and thought. (2) The systematic scheme which defines the interactions of signals in the design of an automatic data-processing system. (3) The basic principles and application of truth tables and interconnection between logical elements required for arithmetic computation in an automatic data-processing system.

LOOP - (1) A self-contained series of instructions in which the last instruction can modify and repeat itself until a terminal condition is reached. The productive instructions in the loop generally manipulate the operands, while bookkeeping instructions modify the productive instructions and keep count of the number of repetitions. A loop may contain any number of conditions for termination. The equivalent of a loop can be achieved by the technique of straight line coding, whereby the repetition of productive and bookkeeping operations is accomplished by explicitly writing the instructions for each repetition. (2) A communications circuit between two private subscribers or between a subscriber and the local switching center.

LPM - Lines Per Minutes.

MACHINE, ELECTRICAL ACCOUNTING - The set of conventional punch card equipment including sorters, collators, and tabulators. Synonymous with EAM.

MAGNETIC CORE - A magnetic core is a small, doughnut-shaped ferroelectric ring, usually about 1/16" in diameter. A bit of information is read into the core by sending current through wires passing through the center of the core. Each core stores only one bit of information at a time, so storage volume depends upon the number of cores used.

MAGNETIC DRUM - A rotating cylinder that has a surface coated with a material on which information may be recorded in small magnetic spots representing binary information.

MAGNETIC TAPE - A long ribbon-like strip of plastic or mylar material which is coated with a metallic substance to store data recorded in magnetized spots.

MATRIX - (1) An array of quantities in a prescribed form; in mathematics, usually capable of being subjected to a mathematical operation by means of an operator or another maxtrix according to prescribed rules. (2) An array of coupled circuit elements, e.g., diodes, wires, magnetic cores, and relays, which are capable of performing a specific function such as conversion from one numerical system to another. The elements are usually arranged in rows and columns. Thus a matrix is a particular type of encoder or decoder.

MEMORY - Synonymous with storage.

MERGE - To combine items from two or more similarly sequenced files into a single file.

MICROSECOND - One millionth of a second (0.000001 second). A time measurement used to measure the operating speed of a computer.

MILLISECOND - One thousandth of a second (0.001 second). A time measurement used to measure the operating speed of a computer.

MODEL, MATHEMATICAL - The general characterization of a process, object, or concept in terms of mathematics which enables the relatively simple manipulation of variables to be accomplished in order to determine how the process, object, or concept would behave in different situations.

NANOSECOND - A billionth of a second (0.000000001 second). A time measurement used to measure the operating speed of a computer.

NOISE - The meaningless extra bits or words which must be ignored or removed from the data at the time the data are used.

OFF-LINE - Descriptive of a system and of the peripheral equipment or devices in a system in which the operation of peripheral equipment is not under the control of the central processing unit. Clarified by equipment, off-line.

ON-LINE - Descriptive of a system and of the peripheral equipment or devices in a system in which the operation of such equipment is under control of the central processing unit (CPU), and in which information reflecting current activity is introduced into the data-processing system as soon as it occurs. Thus, directly in-line with the main flow of transaction processing. Clarified by equipment, on-line.

OPERATION, REAL-TIME - The use of the computer as an element of a processing system in which the times of occurrence of data transmission are controlled by other portions of the system or by physical events outside the system and cannot be modified for convenience in computer programing. Such an operation either proceeds at the same speed as the events being simulated or at a sufficient speed to analyze or control external events happening concurrently.

OPERATIONS RESEARCH (OR) - The use of analytic methods adopted from mathematics for solving operational problems. The objective is to provide management with a more logical basis for making sound predictions and decisions. Among the common scientific techniques used in operations research are the following: linear programing, probability theory, information theory, game theory, Monte Carlo method, and queuing theory.

OPERATOR - (1) A mathematical symbol which represents a mathematical process to be performed on an associated operand. (2) The portion of an instruction which tells the machine what to do. (3) A machine operator.

OPTIMIZATION - A processing method which is continually adjusted to the best obtainable set of operating conditions.

OUTPUT - (1) The information transferred from the internal storage of a computer to secondary or external storage or to any device outside of the computer. (2) The routines which direct (1). (3) The device or collective set of devices necessary for (1). (4) To transfer from internal storage onto external media.

OVERFLOW - The result of an arithmetic operation that exceeds the capacity of the number of positions set aside for the total.

PAPER TAPE - A ribbon-like strip of paper, one inch or less in width, used as a means of recording data in the form of coded perforations.

PARAMETER - (1) A quantity in a subroutine whose value specifies or partly specifies the process to be performed. It may be given different values when the subroutine is used in different main routines or in different parts of one main routine but usually remains unchanged throughout any one such use. (2) A quantity used in a generator to specify machine configuration, designate subroutines to be included, or otherwise describe the desired routine to be generated. (3) A constant or a variable in mathematics which remains constant during some calculation. (4) A definable characteristic of an item, device, or system.

PERIPHERAL EQUIPMENT - Units or devices that are part of an entire data-processing system, but not actually part of a computer; e.g., a Flexo-writer functioning off-line, card sorter, reproducer, forms encoder, external storage unit, printer.

PICOSECOND - One thousandth of a nanosecond, or 10^{-12} seconds; abbreviated psec.

PRINTER - An output device for printing out computer results as numbers, words, or symbols. Can be anything from electric typewriter to high-speed printer.

PRINTER, HIGH-SPEED (NSP) - A printer which operates at a speed more compatible with the speed of computation and data processing so that it may operate on-line.

PRINTER, LINE - A device capable of printing one line of characters across a page, i.e., 100 or more characters, simultaneously as continuous paper advances line by line in one direction past type bars or a type cylinder that contains all characters in all positions.

PROCESSING, DATA - (1) The preparation of source media which contain data or basic elements of information and the handling of such data according to precise rules of procedure to accomplish such operations as classifying, sorting, calculating, summarizing, and recording. (2) The production or records and reports.

PROCESSING, ELECTRONIC DATA (EDP) - Data processing performed largely by electronic equipment. Related to processing, automatic data.

PROGRAM - (1) The complete plan for the solution of a problem; more specifically, the complete sequence of machine instructions and routines necessary to solve a problem. (2) To plan the procedures for solving a problem with the help of a computer. This may involve, among other things, the analysis of the problem, preparation of a flow diagram, preparation of details, testing and development of subroutines, allocation of storage locations, specification of input and output formats, and the incorporation of a computer run into a complete data-processing system. Related to routine. (3) Specific instructions for a computer to determine its operations.

PROGRAM, SOURCE - A computer program written in a language designed for ease of expression of a class of problems or procedures by human beings; e.g., symbolic or algebraic. A generator, assembler, translator, or compiler routine is used to perform the mechanics of translating the source program into an object program in machine language.

PROGRAM TAPE - A magnetic or punched paper tape containing functional or machine instruction codes for a particular application.

PROGRAMING, AUTOMATIC - The method or technique whereby the computer itself is used to transform or translate programing from a language or form that is easy for a human being to produce into a language that is efficient for the computer to carry out. Examples of automatic programing are compiling, assembling, and interpretive routines.

PROGRAMMER - One who prepared specific instructions for a computer to determine its operations and the sequence in which problems are to be solved or data processed.

RAM (Random Access Memory) - A storage technique in which the time required to obtain information is independent of the location of the information most recently obtained. This strict definition must be qualified by the observation that we usually mean "relatively random." Thus, magnetic drums are relatively nonrandom access when compared to magnetic cores for main storage but are relatively random access when compared to magnetic tapes for file storage. Contrasted with storage, sequential access.

READER, CHARACTER - A specialized device which can convert data represented in one of the type fonts or scripts read by human beings directly into machine language. Such a reader may operate optically; or if the characters are printed in magnetic ink, the device may operate magnetically or optically.

REAL-TIME - A method of processing data so fast that there is virtually no passage of time between inquiry and result.

REGISTER - A hardware device used to store a certain amount of bits or characters. Common programming usage demands that a register have the ability to operate upon information and not merely store information; hardware usage does not make the distinction.

RESET - To return a device to zero or to another selected condition.

ROUTINE - A set of coded instructions arranged in proper sequence to direct the computer to perform a desired operation or sequence of operations. A subdivision of a program consisting of two or more instructions that are functionally related; therefore, a program. Clarified by subroutine and related to program.

RUN - The performance of one program on a computer; thus, the performance of one routine or several routines linked so that they form an automatic operating unit, during which manual manipulations by the computer operator are zero or at least minimal.

SCAN - To examine every reference or every entry in a file routinely as a part of a retrieval scheme; occasionally, to collate.

SELECTORS - Automatic switches which give flexibility to a system. They allow the computer to consider a variety of values and pick out the appropriate one.

SENSE - (1) To examine, particularly relative to a criterion. (2) To determine the present arrangement of some element of hardware, especially a manually set switch. (3) To read punched holes or other marks.

SENSING, MARK - A technique for detecting special pencil marks entered in special places on a mark-sense card or on a mark-sense sheet of paper and automatically translating the marks onto a storage device or into punched holes on a computer card.

SET - (1) To place a storage device in a prescribed state. (2) To place a binary cell in the one (1) state. (3) A collection of elements having some feature in common or bearing a certain relation to one another; e.g., in a series, a group of irrational numbers, all positive even integers less than 100 may be a set or a subset.

SHOP, CLOSED - The operation of a computer facility where programming service to the user is the responsibility of a group of specialists, thereby effectively separating the phase of task formulation from that of computer implementation. The programmers are not allowed in the computer room to run or oversee the running of their programs. Contrasted with shop, open.

SHOP, OPEN - The operation of a computer facility where computer programing, coding, and operating can be performed by any qualified employee of the organization, not necessarily by the personnel of the computer center itself, and where the programer may assist in or oversee the running of his program on the computer. Contrasted to shop, closed.

SIMULATION - (1) The representation of physical systems and phenomena by computers, models, or other equipment; e.g., an imitative type of data processing in which an automatic computer is used as a model of some entity. Information enters the computer to represent the factors entering the real process, the computer produces information that represents the results of the process, and the processing done by the computer represents the process itself. (2) In computer programing, the technique of setting up a routine for one computer to make it operate as nearly as possible like some other computer.

SOFTWARE - As opposed to hardware, which refers to the components of a computer system, software is a term applied to program packages furnished by the computer manufacturer of the assembly programs which are adaptable to a specific computer.

SOLID STATE ELEMENTS - Refers to electronic components in computers which use transistors and similar electronic devices instead of vacuum tubes.

SORT - To arrange items of information according to rules dependent upon a key or field contained in the items or records; e.g., to digital sort is to sort first the keys on the least significant digit and to resort on each higher-order digit until the items are sorted on the most significant digit.

STORAGE - (1) The term preferred to memory. (2) Pertaining to a device in which data can be stored and from which they can be obtained at a later time. The means of storing data may be chemical, electrical, or mechanical. (3) A device consisting of electronic, electrostatic, electrical hardware, or other elements on which data may be entered, and from which data may be obtained as desired. (4) The erasable storage in any given computer. Synonymous with memory.

STORAGE, ERASABLE - (1) A storage device whose data can be altered during the course of a computation; e.g., magnetic tape, drum, and cores. (2) An area of storage used for temporary storage.

STORAGE, EXTERNAL - (1) The storage of data on a device which is not an integral part of a computer, but in a form prescribed for use by the computer. (2) A facility or device, not an integral part of a computer, on which data usable by a computer are stored, such as off-line magnetic tape units or punch card devices. Contrasted with storage, internal.

STORAGE, INTERNAL - (1) The storage of data on a device which is an integral part of a computer. (2) The storage facilities forming an integral physical part of the computer and directly controlled by the computer. In such facilities all data are automatically accessible to the computer. Examples are magnetic core and magnetic tape on-line. Contrasted with storage, external.

STORAGE, MAGNETIC DISK - A storage device or system consisting of magnetically coated disks on the surface of which information is stored in the form of magnetic spots arranged in a manner to represent binary data. These data are arranged in circular tracks around the disks and are accessible to reading and writing heads on an arm which can be moved mechanically to the desired disk and then to the desired track on that disk. Data from a given track are read or written sequentially as the disk rotates. Related to storage, disk.

STORAGE, MAGNETIC DRUM - The storage of data on the surface of magnetic drums. Related to drum, magnetic.

STORAGE, MAGNETIC TAPE - A storage device in which data are stored in the form of magnetic spots on metal or coated plastic tape. Binary data are stored as small magnetized spots arranged in column form across the width of the tape. A read-write head is usually associated with each row of magnetized spots so that one column can be read or written at a time as the tape traverses the head.

STORAGE, RANDOM ACCESS - A storage device wherein access to the next position from which information is to be obtained is in no way dependent on the position from which information was previously secured. The opposite of this is sequential access storage, an illustration of which is data stored on a reel of magnetic tape. Same as RAM.

STORAGE, SEQUENTIAL ACCESS - A storage technique in which the terms of information stored become available only in a one-after-the-other sequence whether or not all the information or only some of it is desired. An example is magnetic tape storage. Related to storage, serial, and contrasted with storage, random access.

STORED PROGRAM - A program stored internally in a data-processing system for control of machine function.

SUBROUTINE - (1) The set of instructions necessary to direct the computer to carry out a well-defined mathematical or logical operation. (2) A subunit of a routine. A subroutine is often written in relative or symbolic coding even when the routine to which it belongs is not. (3) A portion of a routine that causes a computer to carry out a well-defined mathematical or logical operation. (4) A routine which is arranged so that control may be transferred to it from a master routine and so that, at the conclusion of the subroutine, control reverts to the master routine. Such a subroutine is usually called a closed subroutine. (5) A single routine may be simultaneously both a subroutine with respect to another routine and a master routine with respect to a third. Usually, control is transferred to a single subroutine from more than one place in the master routine, and the reason for using the subroutine is to avoid having to repeat the same sequence of instructions in different places in the master routine. Clarified by routine.

SYMBOLIC CODE - Instructions for a computer written in a form which is easy for the programmer but must later be converted into machine language, such as COBOL or ALGOL.

SYSTEM - An assembly of procedures, processes, methods, routines, or techniques united by some form of regulated interaction to form an organized whole.

SYSTEM, INFORMATION - The network of all communication methods within an organization. Information may be derived from many sources other than a data-processing unit, such as by telephone, by contact with other people, or by studying an operation.

SYSTEM, INFORMATION RETRIEVAL - A system for locating and selecting, on demand, certain documents or other graphic records relevant to a given information requirement from a file of such material. Examples of information retrieval systems are classification, indexing, and machine-searching systems.

SYSTEM, MANAGEMENT INFORMATION - A communications process in which data are recorded and processed for operational purposes. The problems are isolated for higher-level decision making, and information is fed back to top management to reflect the progress or lack of progress made in achieving major objectives.

TABULATOR - A machine which reads information from one medium -- e.g., cards, paper tape, and magnetic tape -- and produces lists, tables, and totals on separate forms or continuous paper. Synonymous with machine, electrical accounting.

TAPE - A strip of material which may be punched, coated, or impregnated with magnetic or optically sensitive substances and used for data input, storage, or output. The data are stored serially in several channels across the tape transversely to the reading or writing motion.

TAPE, MAGNETIC - A tape or ribbon of any material impregnated or coated with magnetic or other material on which information may be placed in the form of magnetically polarized spots.

THIN-FILM MEMORY - An advanced storage method with very short access time, which uses a film of metallic vapor deposited on a thin glass plate. The film can be magnetized in a billionth of a second.

TIME, REAL - (1) The time it takes a computer to locate data or an instruction word in its storage section and transfer it to its arithmetic unit where the required computations are performed. (2) The time it takes to transfer information which has been operated on from the arithmetic unit to the location in storage where the information is to be stored.

TRANSISTORS - Tiny elements in an electronic circuit that do much the same job as a vacuum tube. They are highly efficient and reliable and generate little heat.

TUBE, CATHODE RAY - (1) An electronic vacuum tube containing a screen on which information may be stored by means of a multigrid modulated beam of electrons from the thermionic emitter storage effected by means of charged or uncharged spots. (2) A storage tube. (3) An oscilloscope tube. (4) A picture tube.

TUBE, DISPLAY - A cathode ray tube used to display information.

UPDATING - The act of bringing information up to the current time or value.

UTILITY PROGRAM - A standard routine used to assist in the operation of the computer; e.g., a conversion routine, a sorting routine, a print-out routine, or a tracing routine.

VARIABLE - (1) A quantity which can assume any of the numbers. (2) A condition, transaction, or event which changes or may be changed as a result of processing additional data through the system.

VARIABLE DATA - Data or information which is, or is assumed to be, changing.

VARIABLE WORD LENGTH - Refers to a storage device in which the capacity for digits or characters in each unit of data is a variable length. This conserves storage space because a 4-digit field will take only 4 positions in a variable length system but might take up 10 positions in a fixed-length storage device.

VIRTUAL MEMORY - A technique that permits the user to treat secondary (disk) storage as an extension of core-memory, thus giving the virtual appearance of a larger core memory.

APPENDIX B

EDP Chronology

1642 - Blaise Pascal invents first mathematical digital calculator, better known as an adding machine.

1694 - Stepped-wheel calculator developed by Gottfried Wilhelm von Leibnitz is capable of performing all four arithmetic functions.

1804 - Joseph Marie Jacquard perfects first punched card machine; used to weave intricate designs into cloth.

1812 - Charles P. Babbage, professor of mathematics at Trinity College, Cambridge, England, thought of building a difference engine, capable of automatically computing mathematical tables.

1822 - Model of the difference engine completed by Babbage, receiving wide attention for the feat.

1829 - Charles Xavier Thomas of Colmar, France, designs a calculator which is said to be the first to perform all four mathematical functions correctly.

1834 - Babbage designed and partially built the "analytical engine," the first completely automatic general purpose digital computer.

1871 - Babbage dies before analytical engine is completed.

1872 - Frank Stephen Baldwin and Charles Xavier Thomas have similar idea for a calculator. Beginning of the calculating machine industry in the U.S.A.

1880 - Dr. Herman Hollerith, statistician, is employed by the U.S. Census Bureau to speed up the processing of census data. Manual tabulating methods were used for this census and took seven and a half years.

1887 - A system using the punched card principal is completed by Hollerith. It was the first machine using paper strips with holes punched into them. Eventually, 3 x 5-in. corner-cut cards, a punch, a pin press, electro-magnetic counters and a sorting box were developed for the system.

1887 - Dorr Eugene Felt patents his comptometer.

1890 - Using Dr. Hollerith's punched card principle, this census was completed in two and a half years.

1889 - The first practical adding and listing (printing) machines were produced by Felt.

1892 - A 90-key machine with a capacity of nine decimal digits is developed by W. S. Burroughs.

1896 - Dr. Hollerith organizes Tabulating Machine Co. to develop his machines for commercial sale.

1901 - The basic numerical punch keyboard and other system improvements are introduced by Hollerith.

1901 - In 200 feet of water off Greek island of Antikythera, divers find an analog type of computer that dated from the first century B.C.

1908 - James Powers, statistician, produces a die-set punch capable of punching 20-column cards on a simultaneous punching principle.

1910 - About 300 punches, related sorters and tabulators manufactured by Powers were installed for the census.

1911 - Dr. Hollerith's Tabulating Machine Co. merged with International Time Recording Co. and Dayton Scale Co. to form the Computing-Tabulating Recording Co.

1914 - Dr. Hollerith retires and Thomas J. Watson, Sr. becomes president of Computing-Tabulating Recording Co.

1914 - A 10-key adding machine is produced by Oscar and David Sundstrand.

1914 - The Monroe calculator is invented by James R. Monroe and Frank S. Baldwin. Although considered a nonprinting device, it went beyond simple adding machine functions in that it could multiply and divide automatically at much greater speeds than other devices of that time.

1915 - Ford Instrument Co. developed the first analog computer.

1924 - Computing-Tabulating Recording Co. changes its name to International Business Machines Corp.

1927 - Powers Accounting Machine Co. merges with other supply companies to form Remington Rand Corp.

1936 - First large IBM installation took place at U.S. Social Security. IBM punched card equipment would be able to perform 120 million postings a year.

1937 - Prof. Howard Aiken of Harvard became interested in combining some established principles with punched cards pioneered by Dr. Hollerith and James Powers to build an automatic calculating device.

1941 - Karl Zuse completed the first program-controlled computer.

1944 - With the cooperation of IBM, the Mark I was built and presented to Harvard. It was an automatic sequence-controlled calculator designed by Prof. Aiken.

1945 - Dr. J. von Neumann wrote the first program for EDVAC, an internal sorting routine. It consisted of the rearrangement of numbers in ascending sequences in an attempt to prove that computers could be used in projects other than those of a scientific nature.

1946 - Dr. John W. Mauchly and J. Presper Eckert used the facilities at the Moore School of Electrical Engineering, University of Pennsylvania, to design and build ENIAC (Electronic Numerical Integrator and Calculator). It contained no moving parts other than input/output gear.

1946 - Eckert and Mauchly leave University of Pennsylvania to form Electronic Control Co.

1948 - Bell Laboratories develop the transistor.

1949 - BINAC, the first computer to use the principle of complete internal self-checking, was developed.

1949 - EDSAC becomes the first stored-program electronic digital computer ever to operate. It was developed by Dr. Maurice V. Wilkes, director of the Mathematical Laboratory, Cambridge University.

1950 - Engineering Research Associates delivers first stored-program scientific computers to U.S. Navy and to Georgia Institute of Technology. Later named the Univac 1101, this computer stored a program and data around the surface of a rotating magnetic drum.

1951 - Univac I, world's first commercial computer was dedicated at U.S. Bureau of Census. This first commercially stored-program electronic computer utilized a mercury delay line internal storage. The 16,000-pound central processor had over 5,000 vacuum tubes and could perform approximately 1,000 calculations per second.

1951 - Maurice V. Wilkes, David J. Wheeler and Stanley Gill authored the first book on programming, <u>The Preparation of Programs for an Electronic Digital Computer</u>, Addison-Wesley Publishing Co., Reading, Mass.

1953 - Univac 1103, an improved version of the Univac 1101, was first computer with coincident current magnetic core storage. It was about 2,000 times faster than the 1101 and 50 times faster than Univac I.

1953 - The first production model of the IBM 701 electronic calculator was set up at the world headwuarters of IBM in New York City. It was 25 times faster in over-all speed but less than one-fourth the size of IBM's selective sequence electronic calculator. The 701 used all three memory devices of the time: cathode ray tubes, magnetic drums and magnetic tape.

1954 - IBM developed the first punched card transmitter that "talks" over regular telephone circuits. The IBM transceiver operated at the rate of approximately 1,000 alphabetical or numeric characters a minute.

1954 - The first Burroughs 205 was delivered. It had a 4K drum storage concurrent magnetic tape search and a buffered printer on-line.

1954 - National Cash Register Co. introduced CRC 102D general purpose computer which had the ability to accept data from an electric typewriter, punched paper tape, magnetic tape or punched cards. The paper tape reader read 200 characters per second and the paper tape punch operated at 60 characters per second.

1954 - IBM showed the 702 electronic data processing system with a 1,000-word electrostatic storage. Up to 6,000 words could be accommodated on each drum. It could process information tape-to-cards at the rate of 100 cards per minute and could print from tape at 150 lines per minute.

1955 - IBM installed its first 702 computer.

1955 - Remington Rand merged with Sperry Gyroscope Co. to form Sperry Rand Corp.

1955 - Type 740 cathode ray tube output recorded was designed by IBM for use with 701 electronic data processing machines. It could record computer data-points on two CRT faces at the rate of 8,000 points a second.

1955 - Univac II magnetic core electronic computer had a regular memory of 24,000 characters. Up to 120,000 characters of information could be stored in core memory.

1955 - The Univac Division of Sperry Rand introduced the Univac 120 punched card computer.

1955 - First IBM 704 computer is delivered.

1956 - Intelligent Machines Research Corp. installs a Scandex optical character reader at Reader's Digest. This was the first paying commercial installation of such a unit.

1956 - IBM installs its first 705 computer.

1956 - Univac delivers the first solid state computer employing no vacuum tubes to Cambridge Air Research Center.

1956 - IBM unveiled electrostatic card printer and electrostatic label printer, both using the principle of Xerographic reproduction.

1957 - Backus and others develop FORTRAN for use with the IBM 704. Other software by different developers included UNICODE for the Univac 1103A and 1105, APT (Automatically Programmed Tools), and IPL-V for the IBM 650 (Newell, Shaw and Simon).

1957 - Control Data Corp. established.

1957 - The first Univac II was delivered. The 2K core computer had a storage cycle time of 40 microseconds.

1957 - Datamatic Div., Honeywell installs the first D-1000, a 50-ton vacuum tube computer system that used 26-pound, three-inch-wide magnetic tape.

1958 - New software included ALGOL, NELIAC (Navy Electronics Laboratory International ALGOC Compiler) and Commercial Translator (for the IBM 709).

1958 - Friden Calculating Machine Co. designed the Teledata, a machine for sending, receiving and checking data encoded in more than five channels of punched paper tape over existing wire services. The same month, the company introduced the Selectadata, which made it possible for automatic selection and sorting of data encoded in punched tape, eliminating the need for conversion to punched cards within the area of its code capacity.

1958 - IBM developed the 709 electronic data processing machine. It could make up to 2.4 million "decisions' per minute in terms of true-and-false answers and could memorize over one million bits of information. Any word in the memory could be located and made ready for use in 12 millionths of a second.

1958 - Potter Instrument Co. introduced the 3260 alphanumeric printer, which could print up to 28 lines of numbers or up to 10 lines of alphanumerics per second. The maximum printing rate was 1,120 numbers per second.

1958 - IBM delivered its first 709 computer which had a 4-32K core or an 8-16K drum, depending on model.

1958 - Philco delivered its first 2000/210 computer.

1958 - Burroughs installed its first 220 computer, with a basic magnetic core memory of 2,000 words, expandable to 10,000 words in increments of 1,000.

1959 - Honeywell's Datamatic Div. introduced the model 800 computer system, a second generation machine that performed up to eight DP tasks at the same time.

1959 - Sperry Rand developed the Univac solid-state computer, the first magnetic amplified commercial DP system. Its memory consisted of 50,000 characters (alphabetic or numeric) and the printer operated at 600 lines a minute.

1959 - The B251 visible record computer is introduced by Burroughs utilizing MICR (Magnetic Ink Character Recognition). It contained over 4,000 transistors.

1959 - GE announced the ERMA computerized system for the banking industry. It was developed in conjunction with the Stanford Research Institute and the Bank of America.

1960 - IBM introduced the 1401 data processing system. Available with 1,400 to 2,000 or 4,000 positions of core storage, it could perform 193,300 additions (eight-digit numbers) or 25,000 multiplications (six-digit numbers into four-digit numbers) in one minute.

1960 - Radio Corp. of American unveiled its RCA 501 computer.

1960 - IBM introduced the 1620 data processing system. It had a magnetic core storage of 20,000 digits and could perform more than 100,000 calculations a minute.

1960 - IBM opened its first data center in the Wall Street area of New York City, charging customers for use of computers by the hour.

1960 - COBOL was developed by the Conference on Data Systems Languages and JOVIAL for the IBM 709 by SDC.

1960 - RCA opens an electronic data processing center on Wall Street.

1960 - Control Data Corp. designed the 160 desk size, all-transistorized computer for handling data transmissions to and from input/output equipment at speeds up to 65,000 characters per second. It could execute 60,000 instructions in a second.

1960 - Sperry Rand delivered the first Univac Larc solid-state computer.

1960 - Nation's first data communications network is established by Collins Radio using a punched card transmission system.

1960 - Univac III is introduced by Sperry Rand with a processing speed nine times faster than that of the Univac II. It was the first commercial system capable of operating with more than one program at the same time.

1960 - The PDP-1 by Digital Equipment Corp. and the GE 210 by General Electric were first installed.

1960 - IBM opened its Systems Research Institute at the United Nations Plaza in New York City. This was the first industry-sponsored graduate school to educate people for advanced professional work in systems engineering.

1961 - NCR delivered its first 390 system, the first electronic computer able to read and process a conventional-type business document utilizing magnetic coatings on the back of regular ledger cards.

1961 - Bell Telephone introduced its Dataspeed service for handling up to 1,050 words a minute.

1962 - The first Univac File Computer II was delivered. It had a core memory instead of a drum as on the Univac File Computer I.

1962 - The first 315 computer with a 6,000- to 120,000-character memory was delivered by NCR. It was able to sort checks for banks at speeds up to 180,000 per hour.

1962 - Univac becomes a separate division of Sperry Rand Corp.

1962 - The first Certificate in Data Processing (CDP) Examination is administered by NMAA during its annual meeting which was held during June 19-22 in New York City.

1962 - The Univac 1107 was announced. This was the first commercially available computer that employed a thin film control storage which reduced access time from millionths to billionths of a second.

1962 - The first battery-powered adding machine is introduced by NCR.

1963 - Digital Equipment Corp. delivered its first Programmed Data Processor-5 (PDP-5) computer.

1963 - IBM unveiled the 1240 bank data processing system. The control of sorting was by instructions programmed in the computer.

1964 - General Electric introduced the Compatibles-400 line, the first "family" of computers.

1964 - General Electric unveiled its DIAL COMM system, private industry's first nationwide, desk-to-desk, direct dial communications network.

1964 - Univac announced the 1108 large-scale core storage computer having the capability to do one million calculations per second.

1964 - Burroughs unveiled the B5500 modular electronic data processing system, up to three times more productive capacity-wide than the B5000.

1964 - NCR installed its first 315/100 computer.

1965 - RCA introduced the RCA Spectra 70 series.

1965 - CDC introduced the 6400 computer with an execution speed of one million instructions per second. That same month, the company also showed its 6800 computer, a machine that had an execution speed of 12 million instructions per second.

1965 - Honeywell introduced the Series 200. Operating speeds were three microseconds for the H-120 (smallest unit) to 188 nanoseconds for the H-4200 (largest unit).

1965 - NCR unveiled the Series 500. The basic memory was 2,400 characters and went up to 4,800 characters.

1965 - BASIC was developed at Dartmouth College for the GE 225.

1965 - Mohawk Data Sciences Corp. delivered its first key-to-tape data recorders.

1965 - IBM installed its first System/360, the first commercially available data processing system designed on the use of micro-miniature circuits.

1966 - GE introduced the GE-645 time-sharing system. More than 1,000 terminals may be plugged into the system at one time.

1966 - The CDC 3500 time-sharing computer was developed.

1966 - Sperry Rand announced the Univac 1108-II time-sharing system which provides five times more computing capacity than the original Univac 1108.

1966 - PL/1 was developed for the IBM 360 systems.

1966 - Western Union opened a real-time Information Services Computer Center in New York City linked with its Telex system.

1966 - Sperry Rand unveiled its Univac 9000 series. The 9200 punched card computer had 8,192 bytes of memory and a cycle time of 1.2 microseconds.

1966 - DEC installed its first PDP-9 computer.

1966 - RCA delivered its first Spectra 70/35 computer system.

1966 - Digital Equipment introduced the PDP-10.

1968 - Honeywell introduced the small-scale model 110 computer system in its Series 200 of third generation systems. At the same time the company unveiled eight models of its new Keytape family of keyboard-to-magnetic tape data preparation devices.

1968 - The PDP-8/I computer introduced by Digital Equipment had a core memory of 4096 12-bit words, expandable to 32,768 words.

1968 - IBM introduced the System/360 Model 85.

1968 - Sperry Rand unveiled the Univac 9400.

1968 - Century 100 is introduced by NCR. It had a 16K thin-film rod memory.

1968 - Honeywell introduced the DDP-324 computer, which had two processing units, each with 8,192 24-bit words of private memory that could be expanded to 24,576 words. It also had 8,192 words of shared memory.

1969 - First day telephone users could attach their own switch-boxes, intercommunication and microwave systems to the public network under new American Telephone & Telegraph Co. tariffs. Revisions stemmed from the Federal Communications Commission's June 1968 decision in the so-called Carterfone case. At that time, the FCC ruled that telephone companies could not prohibit attachments of customer equipment merely on the ground that they were not of telephone company manufacture.

1969 - Computer Sciences Corp. becomes the first computer software and information sciences company to be listed on the New York Stock Exchange.

1969 - IBM introduced the System/3, a 96-column card computer.

1970 - Honeywell introduced the small-scale model 115 computer.

1970 - GE introduced the GE-58 small-scale computer.

1970 - IBM announced two versions of the System/370. Model 155 was up to four times the internal operating speed of the System/360 Model 60.

1970 - GE's computer operations merge with Honeywell. The name of the new company is Honeywell Information Systems.

1970 - The first Registered Business Programmer Examination is administered by DPMA.

1970 - IBM introduced the System/370 Model 145, the first computer using a main memory made entirely of monolithic circuits. The main memory capacity, was over one-half million bytes.

1970 - Honeywell Information Systems introduced first new products after its merger with GE's business computer operations -- the 1640 family of time-sharing computer systems.

1971 - RCA announced the closing of its computer mainframe business.

1971 - IBM extends magnetic tape capabilities to the System/3 Model 10 and adds 96 column card capabilities to most of the 360 and 370 series. In addition, the 3270 CRT system will be added to the 3/10 through new software.

1971-75 - i. All companies introducing new models with third plus generation technology. ii. Many existing and new companies introduce a new line of minicomputers. iii. Several companies introduce microcomputers contained on a single 9 3/4 by 5 3/4 inches plastic card. iv. Expansion of time-sharing and service bureaus.

APPENDIX C

Large School System EDP Survey

Birmingham City Schools
Birmingham, Alabama

Mobile Public Schools
Mobile, Alabama

Fresno Unified School District
Fresno, California

Garden Grove Unified School Dist.
Garden Grove, California

Los Angeles Unified School Dist.
Los Angeles, California

Mt. Diablo Unified School Dist.
Concord, California

Oakland Unified School District
Oakland, California

Sacramento City Unified Sch. Dist.
Sacramento, California

San Diego Unified Schools
San Diego, California

San Juan Unified Schools
Carmichael, California

Denver Public Schools
Denver, Colorado

Jefferson County Public Schools
Lakewood, Colorado

Brevard County School Board
Titusville, Florida

School Board of Broward County
Fort Lauderdale, Florida

Dade County Public Schools
Miami, Florida

School Bd. of Hillsborough
  County
Tampa, Florida

Palm Beach Co. School Dist.
West Palm Beach, Florida

School Bd. of Pinellas Co.
Clearwater, Florida

Chicago Board of Education
Chicago, Illinois

Fort Wayne Community Schools
Fort Wayne, Indiana

School City of Gary
Gary, Indiana

Shawnee Mission Public Schs.
Shawnee Mission, Kansas

Jefferson Co. Bd. of Educ.
Louisville, Kentucky

Caddo Parrish School Board
Shreveport, Louisiana

East Baton Rouge Parrish Sch.
  Bd.
Baton Rouge, Louisiana

New Orleans Public Schools
New Orleans, Louisiana

Anne Arundel Co. Public Schs.
Annapolis, Maryland

Baltimore City Public Schs.
Baltimore, Maryland

Baltimore County
Baltimore, Maryland

Montgomery Co. Public Schs.
Rockville, Maryland

Prince George's Co. Pub. Schs.
Upper Marlboro, Maryland

Boston Schools
Boston, Massachusetts

Detroit Board of Education
Detroit, Michigan

Flint Community Schools
Flint, Michigan

St. Louis Public Schools
St. Louis, Missouri

Clark County School District
Las Vegas, Nevada

Albuquerque Public Schools
Albuquerque, New Mexico

Winston-Salem/Forsyth County
Winston-Salem, North Carolina

Neward Board of Education
Newark, New Jersey

Cincinnati Public Schools
Cincinnati, Ohio

Toledo Public Schools
Toledo, Ohio

Tulsa Public School System
Tulsa, Oklahoma

Portland Public Schools
Portland, Oregon

Philadelphia Public Schools
Philadelphia, Pennsylvania

Pittsburgh Public Schools
Pittsburgh, Pennsylvania

School Dist. of Greenville Co.
Greenville, South Carolina

Nashville Davidson County
Nashville, Tennessee

Memphis City Schools
Memphis, Tennessee

Austin Ind. School Dist.
Austin, Texas

Houston Ind. School Dist.
Houston, Texas

Ft. Worth Public Schools
Ft. Worth, Texas

Fairfax Co. Public Sch. Sys.
Fairfax, Virginia

Norfolk City Schools
Norfolk, Virginia

Richmond Public Schools
Richmond, Virginia

Kanawha County Schools
Charleston, West Virginia

Seattle Public Schools
Seattle, Washington

Milwaukee Public Schools
Milwaukee, Wisconsin

APPENDIX D

Selected Computer Companies

Burroughs Corporation
Burroughs Place
Detroit, Michigan 48232

Control Data Corporation
8100 34th Avenue South
Minneapolis, Minnesota 55440

Data General Corporation
Route 9
Southboro, Massachusetts 01772

Digital Equipment Corporation
146 Main Street
Maynard, Massachusetts 01754

Hewlett-Packard
1501 Page Mill Road
Palo Alto, California 94304

Honeywell Incorporated
2701 4th Avenue South
Minneapolis, Minnesota 55408

IBM
Old Orchard Road
Armonk, New York 10504

Litton ABS
Automated Business Systems
600 Washington Avenue
Carlstadt, New Jersey 07072

NCR
The National Cash Register Co.
Main & K Streets
Dayton, Ohio 45409

Olivetti Corp. of America
500 Park Avenue
New York, New York 10022

The Singer Company
30 Rockefeller Plaza
New York, New York 10020

Texas Instruments Inc.
P. O. Box 5474
Dallas, Texas 75222

Wang Laboratories Inc.
836 North Street
Tewksbury, Massachusetts 01876

Xerox Corporation
701 South Aviation Boulevard
El Segundo, California 90245

APPENDIX E

Selected Magazine Listings

AEDS Journal
Association for Educational
  Data Systems
1201 15th Street, N. W.
Washington, D. C. 20036
($10 for non-members)

AEDS Monitor
Same address as above
($15 for non-members, both of
these excellent magazines are
included in the AEDS dues of
$15, the Monitor appears
monthly while the Journal is
issued quarterly)

Business Automation
Business Publications Inc.
288 Park Ave. West
Elmhurst, Ill. 60126
($15, high quality national
magazine that includes periodic
educational supplements)

Communications News
Brookhill Publishing Co.
402 West Liberty Drive
Wheaton, Illinois 60187
($4.50)

Computer Educator
Computer Education Center
1440 Halsted Street
Chicago Heights, Ill. 60411
($6.00)

Computers and Automation
Berkeley Enterprises Inc.
815 Washington St.
Newtonville, Mass. 02160
($15)

Computerworld
797 Washington Street
Newton, Massachusetts 02160
($12.00 weekly)

Data Processing for Education
American Data Processing Inc.
4th Floor, Book Building
Detroit, Michigan 48226
($24, an exorbitant price to
pay considering the small volume
of output, issued monthly)

Datamation
F. D. Thompson Publications Inc.
330 W. 42nd St.
Greenwich, Conn. 06830
($15, free to qualified personnel)

Data Processing Magazine
No. American Publishing Co.
134 N. 13th Street
Philadelphia, Pa. 19107
($8.50)

Educational Technology
Educational News Service
P. O. Box 508
Saddle Brook, N. J. 07662
($10, issued twice a month, this
magazine covers all aspects of
educational technology, an
excellent means of keeping up to
date with timely and sometimes
refreshingly blunt articles)

Journal of Data Management
DPMA
505 Busse Highway
Park Ridge, Illinois 60068
($5.00)

Journal of Educational Data Processing
Educational Systems Corp.
Box 3711 Georgetown Station
Washington, D. C. 20007
($9, $7 for MEDPA members, a
solid high quality magazine
issued on a quarterly basis)

Sabe Data Processor
Dr. E. Dana Gibson
San Diego State College
San Diego, California 92215
($3, issued monthly)

The Office
Office Publications Inc.
73 Southfield Ave.
Stamford, Conn. 06904
($6, source of office applications of data processing.)

APPENDIX F

Flowcharts

A flowchart is a graphical presentation of a sequence of logical steps to follow in order to solve a particular problem. Though the symbols used vary somewhat, the following from IBM are perhaps the most commonly used.

Basic Symbols

Process

Any processing function; defined operation(s) causing change in value, form, or location of information.

Input/Output

General input/output function; information available for processing (input), or recording of processed information (output).

Connector

Connector; Exit to, or entry from, another part of the chart.

Arrowheads

Arrowheads; In linking symbols, these show operations sequence and data flow direction.

Programming Symbols

Decision

A decision or switching-type operation that determines which of a number of alternative paths is to be followed.

Preparation

Instruction modification to change program; set a switch, modify an index register, initialize a routine.

Terminal Interrupt

A terminal point in a flowchart; start, stop, halt, delay, or interrupt. May show exit from a subroutine.

Systems Symbols

Punched Card   Document   Magnetic Tape   Punched Tape

Online Storage

Input/output using any kind of online storage; magnetic tape, drum, disk.

Keying

An operation using a key-driven device such as punching, verifying, typing.

Display

Information display by online indicators, video devices, console printers, plotters, etc.

Manual Input

Information input by online keyboards, switch settings, push buttons.

Manual Operation

⏢ Any offline process (at "human speed") without mechanical aid.

Auxiliary Operation

▢ Offline performance on equipment not under direct control of central processing unit.

Communication Link

⟶ Transmitting information by a telecommunication link.

APPENDIX G

Selected Educational EDP Facilities

Arlington Public Schools
Arlington, Massachusetts
NCR Century 101

Danvers Public Schools
Danvers, Massachusetts
Honeywell Series 200

Hull High School
Hull, Massachusetts
IBM 1130

Masconomet Regional H.S.
Boxford, Massachusetts
IBM 1130

Melrose Public Schools
Melrose, Massachusetts
PDP-8/(E)
EDU System 50

Natick Public Schools
Natick, Massachusetts
IBM 1130

Northeast Regional Vocational H.S.
Wakefield, Massachusetts
Honeywell Series 200

Pawtucket Public Schools
Pawtucket, Rhode Island
IBM 1130

Salem Public Schools
Salem, New Hampshire
IBM System 3 - Mod 10

Waltham Public Schools
Waltham, Massachusetts
Honeywell Series 200

APPENDIX H

Example 1

WHITTIER REGIONAL VOCATIONAL TECHNICAL HIGH SCHOOL

Superintendent-Director   3 Washington Square
                                                Haverhill, Mass. 08130

Assistant to the Director

9 February 1973

Dear Sir:

The Whittier Regional Vocational Technical School District is issuing a request for a bid specification. It is requested that 5 copies of the bid be provided to the Whittier Administrative Office before 10:00 A.M., Eastern Standard Time, on March 12, 1973.

The following sections are intended as a guide to assist you in understanding Whittier's data processing requirements.

BACKGROUND

Whittier is a vocational technical school incorporating the following cities and towns:

        HAVERHILL   NEWBURYPORT
        AMESBURY   GEORGETOWN
        GROVELAND   IPSWICH
        MERRIMACK   NEWBURY
        WEST NEWBURY   SALISBURY
        ROWLEY

The school is currently under construction off Interstate U.S. Route 495 in Haverhill, Massachusetts. It will have an initial enrollment of 1500 coeducational students in the secondary and the post-secondary levels, incorporating the grade levels of 9 through 14 inclusive. Data Processing initially will enroll 40 students in the post-secondary level and eventually offer a course in the secondary level.

The major intent of the Data Processing Department is the education of students for the data processing field. The graduating student should have a level of competence equal to a Junior Systems Analyst. As an adjunct of our educational process, it is expected that machine time will be available for administrative applications and municipal applications. The opening date of Whittier is September, 1973.

Delivery and installation of all hardware equipment must be accomplished by August 13, 1973, or at a date designated by the Whittier Regional Vocational Technical High School Committee, in writing, prior to July 13, 1973.

Vendor supported and contracted software systems will be operational by August 13, 1973. Test time shall commence April 1, 1973, and shall be continuously available until delivery and installation of all hardware at no expense to Whittier Regional Vocational Technical High School District providing it is within the allowable line.

The Data Processing Department's educational specifications require the offering of training in the batch processing environment. (See specifications for hardware requirements.)

GENERAL

The vendor will consult, recommend, or comment in the various areas of concern upon request.

Enclosed is a separate listing of Applications Programs Systems or User Developed Systems to be included in the contract upon request. (Enclosure I).

The vendor will provide actual computer printouts of the various proposed software systems, along with the necessary documentation for file layouts within 30 days after contractual agreement.

The proposed software systems are to be demonstrable to the administrative staff of Whittier by June 1, 1973.

Accompanying the bids will be a proposed form contract of the necessary systems bid.

HARDWARE (See attachment).

Vendors will configure a system which incorporates all features set forth in the attached bid form, namely: 1-7.

The system will be capable of immediate or future expansion into a multi-programming environment. Automatic restart, hardware bootstrap, operating system executive are desirable features, but not required.

SOFTWARE

A complete line of software application programs now available and in current operation at the vendors' customer sites is desirable. It is expected that these programs will be made available to Whittier, along with the appropriate documentation. Software charges (if any) for the required software systems and necessary operational software will be outlined in detail.

EDUCATION

The vendor will state separately from the bid form the courses required for the training of the Data Processing staff and any additional training for members of Whittier's professional staff. Each course listed shall have a synopsis of its content, duration of course, location taught and costs of the course, plus related costs, i.e., texts, materials, transportation, lodging, meals, and other expenses.

Any contract shall include courses for the training of Whittier's professional staff from the shop and academic areas during the term of the contract. Should Whittier provide a group of such individuals, the vendor must be able to furnish an on-site instructor(s) to meet this need.

APPLICATIONS

A separate listing entitled, "Whittier Requirements" is attached. (See Listing.)

Software systems will be acceptable and operational by August 15, 1973.

The optional systems section contain systems which are expected to be implemented within a 5-year period.

All current software systems now in operation at the vendor's customers' sites shall be available to the Whittier Regional Vocational Technical High School District upon request, together with any requested documentation.

Any costs associated with the software system will be detailed.

SUPPORT

Whittier will be assured that the vendor has the necessary personnel to provide the support needed for our successful installation and operation. Whittier will expect the vendor to comment to this end. Appropriate information regarding the personnel to be used by the vendor in the installation, operation, and support of hardware and software systems shall be furnished with this bid form.

In this connection every bidder should take into consideration the fact that the systems shall be used as educational tools and every bidder should familiarize itself with the educational philosophy set forth in the Whittier Regional Vocational Technical High School District's "Educational Specifications" and a copy of the applicable sections are available upon written request.

The Whittier Regional Vocational Technical High School Committee reserves the right to reject any and all bids.

Any questions concerning the above information should be directed to:

Data Processing Coordinator

SIGNED:

SCHOOL COMMITTEE
WHITTIER REGIONAL VOCATIONAL TECHNICAL HIGH SCHOOL DISTRICT

WHITTIER REGIONAL VOCATIONAL TECHNICAL HIGH SCHOOL DISTRICT

Sealed bids for contract of the following services and equipment will be received at the office of Whittier Regional Vocational Technical High School, 3 Wash. Sq., Haverhill, MA, Rm. 410, until March 12, 1973, at 10 A.M., E.S.T., at which time each bid will be publicly opened and read.

Specifications may be obtained at the office of Whittier Regional Vocational Technical High School, 3 Wash. Sq., Haverhill, MA during usual business hours.

ELECTRONIC DATA PROCESSING EQUIPMENT AND COMPUTER SYSTEM

Each bid shall be accompanied by a certified check for Five Hundred and no/100 ($500.) Dollars payable to Whittier Regional Vocational Technical High School District as liquidated damages on failure of the bidder to sign a contract within seven days after notice of acceptance of bid, or other default.

The successful bidder will be required to furnish a performance and payment bond in the amount of 100% of the contract, the form of the bond and surety company under the bond to be in accordance with the law approved by the school counsel.

Each bid shall be enclosed in a sealed envelope addressed to Representative, W.R.V.T.H.S.D., Haverhill, MA and marked as "BID FOR ELECTRONIC DATA PROCESSING EQUIPMENT AND COMPUTER SYSTEM."

The W.R.V.T.H.S. acting through its agents, reserve the right to reject any or all bids. Bidders shall enclose a brief statement with their bids as to their experience and competence to perform this work.

Business Manager
Whittier Regional Vocational
Technical High School District

HARDWARE

1. Central Processing Unit
2. Memory Size
3. Card Reader
4. Line Printer
5. Disk Units
6. Input-Output Typewriter/printer
7. Tape Drives - 15 KB Transfer Rate Minimum
8.* Card Punch - 60 CPM Minimum
9. Other Recommended Devices

*Optional Device

WHITTIER REGIONAL VOCATIONAL TECHNICAL HIGH SCHOOL DISTRICT

Sealed bids for contract of the following services and equipment will be received at the office of Whittier Regional Vocational Technical High School, 3 Wash. Sq., Haverhill, MA, Rm. 10, until March 12, 1973, at 10 A.M., E.S.T., at which time each bid will be publicly opened and read.

Specifications may be obtained at the office of Whittier Regional Vocational Technical High School, 3 Wash. Sq., Haverhill, MA during usual business hours.

ELECTRONIC DATA PROCESSING EQUIPMENT AND COMPUTER SYSTEM

Each bid shall be accompanied by a certified check for five hundred and no/100 ($500.) Dollars payable to Whittier Regional Vocational Technical High School District as liquidated damages on failure of the bidder to sign a contract within seven days after notice of acceptance of bid, or other default.

The successful bidder will be required to furnish a performance and payment bond in the amount of 100% of the contract the form of the bond and surety company under the bond to be in accordance with the law approved by the school counsel.

Each bid shall be enclosed in a sealed envelope addressed to Representative, W.R.V.T.H.S.D., Haverhill, MA and marked "BID FOR ELECTRONIC DATA PROCESSING EQUIPMENT AND COMPUTER SYSTEM."

The W.R.V.T.H.S. acting through its agents, reserve the right to reject any or all bids. Bidders shall enclose a brief statement with their bids as to their experience and competence to perform this work.

Business Manager
Whittier Regional Vocational
Technical High School District

BID FORM FOR FURNISHING AND INSTALLING AN ELECTRONIC DATA PROCESSING SYSTEM

I. HARDWARE	SYSTEM PROPOSED	SPEED/CAPACITY	MONTHLY RENTAL	ANNUAL COST
1. 1 Central Processing Unit				
2. Memory Size				
3. 1 Card Reader - 300 CPM Minimum				
4. 1 Line Printer - 400 LPM Minimum				
5. 2 Disk Units - Capacity Open				
6. 1 Input-Output Console writer/printer				
7. 3 Tape Drives - 15 KB Transfer 9 Track or Channel Rate Minimum				
*8. 1 Card Punch - 60 CPM Minimum				
9. Other Recommended Devices				

TOTAL MONTHLY AND ANNUAL COST FOR HARDWARE $

*Optional Device

Determine the benefits of mixed tape/disk configuration. Consider the possibility of adding only one tape to the system for back-up purposes. It is much less expensive to store historical information on tape than on disc.

Make the console an optional device. It is not required for efficient operation on most systems.

(SHOULD YOU CARE TO PROPOSE ANY OPTIONAL SYSTEMS, USE THE SAME HEADINGS AS ABOVE AND MARK OPTIONAL.)

SPACE FOR ANY ADDITIONAL INFORMATION PERTAINING TO HARDWARE PROPOSAL:

(PLEASE OUTLINE IN SAME FORMAT.)

SPACE FOR ANY ADDITIONAL INFORMATION PERTAINING TO LANGUAGE SOFTWARE:

SOFTWARE - LANGUAGE	ONE TIME CHARGES OR NO CHARGES	MONTHLY RENTAL	ANNUAL COST
1. FORTRAN			
2. COBOL			
3. R.P.G. or equivalent			
4. BASIC or equivalent			
5. Compiler to Assembler program			
6. Others -- Please List			
TOTAL MONTHLY AND ANNUAL COST OF LANGUAGE SOFTWARE		$	$

SPACE FOR ANY ADDITIONAL INFORMATION PERTAINING TO LANGUAGE SOFTWARE:
(PLEASE OUTLINE IN SAME FORMAT.)

SPACE FOR ANY ADDITIONAL INFORMATION PERTAINING TO HARDWARE PROPOSAL:
(PLEASE OUTLINE AS THE SAME HEADINGS AS ABOVE MARK AND EXPOSE ANY OPTIONAL SYSTEMS, USE THE SAME HEADINGS AS ABOVE AND MARK "OPTIONAL".)

SHOULD YOU CARE TO PROPOSE ANY ADDITIONAL OPTIONAL SYSTEMS, USE THE SAME HEADINGS AS ABOVE AND MARK "OPTIONAL".

Make the console an option device. It is not required for efficient operation of most systems.

Historical information on tape than tape on disc.

Considerations for back-up purposes. It is much less expensive to maintain a mixed tape/disk configuration. Consider the possibility of

SOFTWARE - LANGUAGE	YES OR NO ONE TIME CHARGE	MONTHLY RENTAL	ANNUAL COST
1. FORTRAN		$ _____	$ _____
2. COBOL	_____	_____	_____
3. R.P.G. or equivalent	_____	_____	_____
4. BASIC or equivalent	_____	_____	_____
5. Compiler or Assembler Programs	_____	_____	_____
6. Others -- Please List	_____	_____	_____
	_____	_____	_____
	_____	_____	_____

TOTAL MONTHLY AND ANNUAL COST OF LANGUAGE SOFTWARES

II. SUPPORT

1. Maintenance Support

   A. Labor Cost per Hour   B. Material Cost   C. Availability Hours   D. Availability Days   E. Back-up System Location

   R_____ $_____ $_____ $_____ $_____

SPACE FOR ANY ADDITIONAL INFORMATION PERTAINING TO MAINTENANCE SUPPORT:

2. System Engineering Support

   A. Number of hours Furnished Free _____

   B. Cost per hour if on a Charge Basis _____

   C. Availability Hours _____

   D. Availability Days _____

   E. Location of System Engineering Support _____

   F. Estimate of Total Cost for System Engineering Support for modifications of the following Program Packages:

   INVENTORY CONTROL $ _____

   ENCUMBERANCE ACCOUNTING $ _____

   PAYROLL ACCOUNTING $ _____

   STUDENT ACCOUNTING $ _____

   STUDENT GRADE REPORTING $ _____

   STUDENT SCHEDULING $ _____

SPACE FOR ANY ADDITIONAL INFORMATION PERTAINING TO SYSTEM ENGINEERING SUPPORT:

SOFTWARE - PACKAGE	YES OR NO SUPPORTED	YES OR NO GUARANTEED	*SAMPLE PACKAGE SUBMITTED WITH PROPOSAL (YES OR NO)	YES OR NO OVERTIME CHARGE	ANNUAL COST
III.					
A. Payroll Accounting					
1. Payroll Register					$
2. Check Printing					
3. Quarterly Reports					
4. Deduction Programming					
5. Year-to-date Register					
6. W-2 Forms					
7. End of Year Financial Reports					
8. Teacher Annuities Deductions					
9. Personnel Reports					
10. Weekly Time Sheets					
11. Labor Distribution Report					

*If answer is No, please explain.

	YES OR NO SUPPORTED	YES OR NO GUARANTEED	*SAMPLE PACKAGE SUBMITTED WITH PROPOSAL (YES OR NO)	YES OR NO OVERTIME CHARGE	ANNUAL COST
B. Student Accounting					
1. Satisfying Laws of Comm. of Massachusetts					$
2. Recorded Attendance Report - teacher proof summarizing attendance transactions monthly.					
3. Attendance Register (State Report) - providing average attendance, average membership, and percentage of membership figures.					
4. Cumulative Attendance Report					
5. Attendance Absence Pattern Analysis Report					
6. School Membership Summary Report - providing breakdown of the number of students by age and sex for each grade.					
7. School System Census Report					
				TOTAL ANNUAL COST FOR STUDENT ACCOUNTING PACKAGE	$

*If answer is No, please explain.

SPACE FOR ANY ADDITIONAL INFORMATION PERTAINING TO STUDENT ACCOUNTING PACKAGE:

C. Student Grade Reporting

	YES OR NO SUPPORTED	YES OR NO GUARANTEED	*SAMPLE PACKAGE SUBMITTED WITH PROPOSAL (YES OR NO)	YES OR NO ONETIME CHANGE	ANNUAL COST
1. Mark Sense Reporting	_____	_____	_____	_____	_____
2. Sample Report Cards including Verbal Reports	_____	_____	_____	_____	_____
3. Rank in Class and Quality Point Average	_____	_____	_____	_____	_____
4. Grade Distribution and Frequency for Class, individual teachers, and individual departments	_____	_____	_____	_____	_____
5. Failure List	_____	_____	_____	_____	_____
6. Honor Roll List	_____	_____	_____	_____	_____
7. End of Year Tabulating Labels	_____	_____	_____	_____	_____
8. Attendance Marking period-Cumulative	_____	_____	_____	_____	_____
9. Credits, Current, Cumulative	_____	_____	_____	_____	_____

*If Answer is No, please explain.

C. Student Grade Reporting

	YES OR NO SUPPORTED	YES OR NO GUARANTEED	*SAMPLE PACKAGE SUBMITTED WITH PROPOSAL (YES OR NO)	YES OR NO ONETIME CHANGE	ANNUAL COST
10. Graduating Credit Deficiency Report - provides Guidance Department with list of students who fail to obtain minimum graduating credits					$
11. Capability to provide Weighted and Non-weighted grades					

*If Answer is No, please explain.

TOTAL ANNUAL COST FOR STUDENT GRADE REPORTING $ _____

			*SAMPLE PACKAGE SUBMITTED WITH PROPOSAL (YES OR NO)		
NUMBER	YES OR NO SUPPORTED	YES OR NO GUARANTEED		YES OR NO ONETIME CHANGE	ANNUAL COST

D. <u>Student Scheduling</u>

1. Course Tally $ ____
2. Conflict Matrix for All Courses and Singleton Courses
3. Room Utilization
4. Teacher Utilization
5. Daily Study Hall Assignments
6. Home Room Class & Study Hall Lists
7. Overlapping Schedules
8. Sex Balance
9. Alternate Courses
10. Student Request
11. Seat Availability List
12. Scheduling Statistics

	NUMBER	YES OR NO SUPPORTED	YES OR NO GUARANTEED	*SAMPLE PACKAGE SUBMITTED WITH PROPOSAL (YES OR NO)	YES OR NO ONETIME CHANGE	ANNUAL COST
D. Student Scheduling						
13. List of Courses Causing Conflicts		_____	_____		_____	_____
14. Scheduling Reject List		_____	_____		_____	_____
15. Number of Students	_____					
16. Number of Courses	_____					
17. Number of Sections	_____					
18. Number of Periods	_____					
19. Number of Semesters	_____					
20. Available Resources Report Teacher and Room						

*If answer is No, please explain

TOTAL ANNUAL COST FOR STUDENT SCHEDULING PACKAGE $ _____

SPACE FOR ANY ADDITIONAL INFORMATION PERTAINING TO STUDENT SCHEDULING PACKAGE:

	YES OR NO SUPPORTED	YES OR NO GUARANTEED	*SAMPLE PACKAGE SUBMITTED WITH PROPOSAL (YES OR NO)	YES OR NO ONETIME CHARGE	ANNUAL COST
E. Entire Fiscal Accounting System					
Personnel Accounting					
Encumbrance Accounting					
1. Vendor Master List					
2. Budget Transaction Report					
3. Cash Listing					
4. Purchase Order Transaction Listing					
5. Detailed Budget Report					
6. Cash Statement					
7. Invoice Listing					
8. Bill List					
9. Check Register					
10. Check/Warrant Printing					
11. Vendor Master File Maintenance Report					
Program Budgeting System					
1. Code Book - lists of program, state and object codes and descriptions					
2. Budget Report - listing of all appropriations run at beginning of fiscal year					

*If answer is No, please explain.

	YES OR NO SUPPORTED	YES OR NO GUARANTEED	*SAMPLE PACKAGE SUBMITTED WITH PROPOSAL (YES OR NO)	YES OR NO ONETIME CHARGE	ANNUAL COST
E. Entire Fiscal Accounting System					
3. Weekly Activity Report - shows all PPBS activity by fund, program, locations, state, object and levels showing appropriations, encumbrances, expenditures and unencumbered balances.					
4. Monthly Appropriation Journal - detail report of the entire PPBS Master File.					
5. Monthly Appropriation Report - summary of appropriations, encumbrances, expenditures and unencumbered balances by program within level codes.					
6. Department Head Encumbrance Report - listing by department head of appropriations, encumbrances, expenditures, and unencumbered balances.					
7. Open Purchase Order Report - listing of all purchase orders on PPBS Master File which have not been disencumbered in fund, vendor name, and P.O. number sequence.					

E. Entire Fiscal Accounting System	YES OR NO SUPPORTED	YES OR NO GUARANTEED	*SAMPLE PACKAGE SUBMITTED WITH PROPOSAL (YES OR NO)	YES OR NO ONETIME CHARGE	ANNUAL COST
8. Liability Report - an open P.O. report in fund, state and P.O. number sequence.					$ _____
9. Monthly Budget Summary - listing by state account number showing appropriations, encumbrances, expenditures, abatements, and unencumbered balances.					
10. Monthly Financial Report - by function showing appropriations, encumbrances, expenditures and total with related financial information at bottom of report.					
Inventory Accounting					
Other: _____	_____	_____	_____	_____	_____

*If answer is No, please explain.

TOTAL ANNUAL COST FOR FISCAL ACCOUNTING SYSTEM PACKAGE $ _____

SPACE FOR ANY ADDITIONAL INFORMATION PERTAINING TO FISCAL ACCOUNTING SYSTEM:

F. Student Information System

	YES OR NO SUPPORTED	YES OR NO GUARANTEED	*SAMPLE PACKAGE SUBMITTED WITH PROPOSAL (YES OR NO)	YES OR NO ONETIME CHARGE	ANNUAL COST
1. Student Information					$

*If answer is No, please explain.

TOTAL ANNUAL COST FOR STUDENT INFORMATION PACKAGE

2. Vendor will be responsible for submitting a system layout of the configuration of the computer system equipment and an electrical schematic drawing prior to installation.

SPACE FOR ANY ADDITIONAL INFORMATION PERTAINING TO STUDENT INFORMATION SYSTEM:

IV. GROWTH CAPABILITIES

1. Describe in detail growth capabilities of proposed system:

V. INSTALLED SYSTEM

1. List installed computer systems similar to and compatible with the system proposed.

LOCATION	EQUIPMENT	PROGRAM

EDUCATION OF WHITTIER'S PROFESSIONAL STAFF

COURSES AVAILABLE	COURSE COSTS	OTHER COSTS	TIME & PLACE AVAILABLE	ON-SITE INSTRUCTION COST	OTHER

SPACE FOR ANY ADDITIONAL INFORMATION PERTAINING TO STUDENT EDUCATIONAL SYSTEM:

WHITTIER REQUIREMENTS

SOFTWARE SYSTEMS:

STUDENT SCHEDULING	1500 STUDENTS IN MODULAR FORM
STUDENT RECORDS	STUDENT INFORMATION FILE REPORT CARDS TEST SCORES GUIDANCE REPORTS ATTENDANCE CENSUS INFORMATION STATE & FEDERAL REPORTS
PAYROLL	PROFESSIONAL STAFF NON-PROFESSIONAL PERSONNEL RECORDS PERSONNEL ATTENDANCE
INVENTORY SYSTEM	MOVABLE EQUIPMENT (NON-SERIAL NUMBERED) FIXED EQUIPMENT SERIAL NUMBERED EXPENDABLE EQUIPMENT
FINANCIAL PPBS REQUIREMENTS	WARRANTS ENCUMBRANCES PAYABLES BUDGETARY PROGRAM OPERATING EXPENSES
MAINTENANCE SYSTEM	MAJOR PREVENTATIVE OPERATING AND DAILY MAINTENANCE

OPTIONAL SYSTEMS:	BUS SCHEDULING OR ROUTING
	   BUS LISTINGS
	   ROUTE SCHEDULING
	   OPTIMUM LOADING
	MUNICIPAL APPLICATION SYSTEMS
	WATER BILLING
	REAL ESTATE TAX BILLING
	CENSUS
	VOTER REGISTRATION & LISTINGS
	CASH, CHECK, RECONCILIATION - TREASURERS' OFFICE
	MUNICIPAL ELECTRIC LIGHT DEPARTMENT
	DEPARTMENT OF PUBLIC WORKS
	LAW ENFORCEMENT PROGRAM
	FIRE DEPARTMENT STATISTICAL REPORTING
	ASSESSORS' OFFICE
	   DEED CONTROL
	   LOT PLANNING & ZONING

OPTIONAL SYSTEMS: HEALTH DEPARTMENT
                    RECORDINGS & RETRIEVAL
                    LICENSING COMMISSION
                    LICENSE CONTROL

DATA PROCESSING OBJECTIVES

1. TO GRADUATE AN EMPLOYABLE STUDENT

2. TO HAVE A STUDENT COMPREHEND THE FOLLOWING:

     OPERATING SYSTEMS
     DATA BASE
     MACHINE ARCHITECTURE
     CARD FORMATTING
     TAPE LAYOUTS
     DISK CONCEPTS
     MACHINE ASSEMBLERS
     COMPILERS & LANGUAGES
       RPG
       RPG II
       COBOL
       FORTRAN IV
       BASIC
       PL/1
     FILES DESIGN
     SYSTEMS DESIGN
     DATA ENTRY
     DATA ENTRY DEVICES
     MACHINE OPERATIONS PROCEDURES
     MULTI-PROGRAMMING CONCEPTS
     MULTI-PROCESSING CONCEPTS
     QUEUEING TECHNIQUES
     DATA BASE MANIPULATIONS
     CONVERSION TECHNIQUES
     I/O CONTROL OPERATIONS
     CROSS FOOTING TECHNIQUES
     DATA CONTROL
     SORTING TECHNIQUES
     TURN-AROUND DOCUMENTS
     DOCUMENT DESIGN TECH
     FORMS PLANNING TECH
     FORMS LAYOUT TECH

3. TO HAVE THE STUDENT ACHIEVE THE LEVEL OF A COMPETENT JUNIOR COBOL PROGRAMMER

4. TO HAVE THE STUDENT BECOME A PROFICIENT MACHINE OPERATOR

5. TO PERFORM THE NECESSARY ADMINISTRATIVE FUNCTIONS OF THE SCHOOL DISTRICT

6. TO INVOLVE THE SECONDARY LEVEL IN DATA PROCESSING THROUGH:

    TERMINALS
    EXPOSURE TO MACHINE OPERATIONS
    PROGRAMS OF RELATED STUDY AREAS
    BASIC LANGUAGE
    FORTRAN IV LANGUAGE
    TOOLS OF EDUCATION IN TRADE AREAS
      i.e. - PATTERN DESIGN
           RECIPE RECALL
           AUTOMOBILE JOB CONTROL
           NUMERICAL LATHE MACHINE
             PROGRAMMING
           ETC.

EXAMPLE 2

ANYTOWN PUBLIC SCHOOLS
ANYTOWN, SOMESTATE

NOTICE TO BIDDERS

Sealed proposals are invited and will be received at the Office of the Assistant Superintendent for Data Processing of the Anytown Public Schools, 24 Main Street, Anytown, Somestate until 9:30 A.M., Friday, August 31, 1975, at which place and time they will be publicly opened and read for furnishing and installing an

ELECTRONIC DATA PROCESSING SYSTEM
FOR ANYTOWN PUBLIC SCHOOLS

in accordance with the following specifications. The quoted terms are to include:

A. Lease for a period not to exceed five years.

B. Lease to purchase plan not to exceed five years.

C. Complete purchase.

Specifications and Proposal Forms may be obtained at the Office of the Assistant Superintendent for Data Processing.

Proposals are to be submitted in duplicate in a sealed envelope that is marked appropriately on the outside with the name and address of the vendor, the title of the proposal and the scheduled time, date and location of the opening of proposals.

The Anytown School Board, Awarding Authority, reserves the right to reject any and all proposals, to waive any informalities and to accept a proposal which it considers to serve the best interests of the City of Anytown, Somestate.

City of Anytown

By: John J. Johns

Superintendent of Schools

ANYTOWN PUBLIC SCHOOLS
ANYTOWN, SOMESTATE

SPECIFICATIONS FOR FURNISHING AND INSTALLING AN
ELECTRONIC DATA PROCESSING SYSTEM

SPECIFICATIONS

These specifications call for a stored program computer system to be used for Instructional and Administrative application. This system must meet the following minimum specifications from both a hardware and software capability. Deviations from the listed specifications are not permitted unless they are so noted, and that the vendor can demonstrate to the satisfaction of the Superintendent of Schools or his designee the ability of the proposed system to be the equal of what has been requested. A written specification must accompany the notation of the deviation. It is to be understood that all specifications, both hardware and software, quoted are minimum specifications. Any additions to these specifications must be noted with justification.

HARDWARE REQUIREMENTS - MINIMUM

    A. Central Processing Unit

       32,000 Bytes

    B. Input/Output Devices

       1. Card Reader - 300 cards per minute

       2. Line Printer - 300 lines per minute alphanumeric, 132 print position

       3. Disk packs and storage drives using ceramic heads with a capacity to store 5 million to 9.8 million Bytes providing on line random access and disk sort capability.

       4. Console Keyboard input/output with ability to produce hard copy for both input and output, which will transmit information to be keyed into the system and provides a means of communicating directly with the computer.

    C. Terminal Teletype and Other Input/Output Equipment
       (Must be capable of being field installed.)

       1. The Central Processing unit must have the capability of supporting a minimum of 10 terminal lines for future educational and administrative use.

       2. System must have ability simultaneously to service

on-line terminals and provide batch processing. Specify memory allocation for such dual environment.

    3. Vendor shall include a list of other input/output equipment which can be presently attached to the proposed system. This list shall include a description of the equipment, a statement as to the software support for the equipment, and a statement of the changes and cost that are required of the proposed equipment to support this additional equipment.

<u>SOFTWARE</u> - Demonstrable Documented programs, written specifically for the equipment proposed and which is fully guaranteed by the Vendor, must accompany all Proposals in the form of sample packages.

  A. <u>Language Capability and Documentation in the Following Areas</u>:

    1. FORTRAN ANSI

    2. COBOL ANSI

    3. R.P.G. or equivalent

    4. BASIC or equivalent

    5. Computer and Assembler program for the above.

  B. <u>Student Accounting Program Systems</u>

    1. <u>Student Grade Reporting</u>

      a. Sample report cards including verbal reports

      b. Rank in class and quality point average

      c. Grade distribution and frequency for class, individual teachers, and individual departments

      d. Failure and eligibility lists

      e. Honor Roll list

      f. Permanent record labels for end-of-year

      g. Year-to-date attendance integration

    2. <u>Student Scheduling</u> (Modular)

      a. Course tally

      b. Conflict Matrix for all courses

c. Room Utilization

d. Teacher utilization

e. Daily Study Hall Assignments

f. Homeroom class and study hall lists

g. Lunchroom assignments

h. Overlapping schedule

i. Sex balancing

j. Alternate courses

k. Seat availability lists

l. Conflict display for individual students, showing areas of conflict

m. List of course causing conflicts

n. Ability to change student scheduling and update class lists, from disk profile without rescheduling entire school

o. Minimum parameters include:

   1) 24 modules

   2) 1000 courses

   3) 99 sections per course

   4) 4000 students

   5) 20 course requests per student

   6) 6-day cycle

   7) 4-semester scheduling

   8) 250 teachers

p. Scheduling reject list

3. <u>Student Attendance</u>

A completely proven package must be made available which meets the legal requirements of the Somestate Department of Education and the Laws of the State of Somestate. The system must be capable of being integrated with the grade reporting package.

4. <u>Test scoring and Analysis</u>

    a. Scoring of all objective-type questions

    b. Analysis of test responses

C. <u>Financial and Personnel Accounting Program System</u>

  1. Payroll Accounting

    a. Payroll Registers

    b. Check printing

    c. Quarterly report

    d. Deduction Programming

    e. Year-to-date register

    f. W2 forms

    g. End-of-year Financial Reports (fiscal year)

    h. Payroll distribution by Accounts
                                     Departments
                                       Type of Personnel

    i. Personnel Accounting

  2. <u>Fiscal Accounting System</u>

    a. Encumbrance and Expenditure Accounting

    b. Program Budgeting System

    c. Budget Analyses

    d. Outstanding Purchase Order control

    e. Inventory accounting

D. <u>Educational Program Systems for Student and Teacher Use</u>

  1. Materials for courses directly involved in the instruction of the use of data processing equipment.

    a. Introduction to Computers

    b. Computer Operations

    c. FORTRAN Programming

    d. COBOL Programming

       e. Basic Programming (or equal)

       f. R.P.G. Programming (or equal)

       g. Systems Design

  2. Computer aided instruction

       a. Problem Solving

       b. Computer oriented Math and Science

       c. Independent Study Research

       d. Computer Assisted Instruction

       e. Other

SUPPORT

Vendor shall submit with his proposal detailed explanations and costs of the following:

1. Maintenance including parts and labor

2. Back-up from other users and Vendor Center

3. Conversion of present payroll package Census system

4. Education of data processing personnel, educational staff and administrative personnel. Include course descriptions, locations, dates and costs. Also include any educational allowance.

5. Systems engineering support. Please include preinstallation and post-installation support as well as pre-installation program test time and location.

6. Manuals and manual up-date service. This should include a detailed library listing of materials and costs with details of procedure for updating of operating manuals and Resident Monitor System.

7. Cost of installation and list of details of any changes physical, electrical, etc., from present computer site.

8. Definition of Supported Software must be given. (The educational support system should allow for special courses for data processing personnel, familiarization courses for administrative personnel and planning for orientation programs for staff and students.)

DELIVERY

The proposal must be made based on a guaranteed delivery and total completed installation date of JANUARY 1, 1976.

PENALTY CLAUSE

Vendor must outline in detail the penalty, if any, should the Anytown School Board and/or the City of Anytown terminate the allocation of funds for the support of the proposed system for any reason prior to the end of the contract time under both Lease, and Lease to Purchase contracts on a 5-year basis.